THE ART OF T. S. ELIOT

THE ART OF
T. S. ELIOT

By

HELEN GARDNER

A Dutton **dep** *Paperback*

Everyman

NEW YORK
E. P. DUTTON & CO., INC.

This paperback edition of
"THE ART OF T. S. ELIOT"
Published 1959 by E. P. Dutton & Co., Inc.
All rights reserved. Printed in the U.S.A.

THE ART OF T. S. ELIOT was first published in 1950.

TO
JANE LANG

PREFACE

THE ORIGIN of this book is an article which appeared first as 'The Recent Poetry of T. S. Eliot' in *New Writing and Daylight* (Summer 1942). It was revised and enlarged to include a study of *Little Gidding* for *Penguin New Writing* (No. 29, 1946), and for inclusion in *T. S. Eliot: A Study of his Writings by Several Hands* edited by Mr B. Rajan (1947). I am grateful to the editors: Mr John Lehmann and Mr Rajan, and to the publishers: The Hogarth Press Ltd, Penguin Books Ltd and Dennis Dobson Ltd for permission to use portions of these articles in the second and final chapters.

The more immediate source is a short course of lectures delivered in the University of Oxford in the spring of 1948. For these lectures and for the writing of this book I did not re-read any of Mr Eliot's critics, but it will be plain that I owe much, even if no definite reference is made, to what I have learnt from them in the past. I should like to make here a general acknowledgment to Professor F. O. Matthiessen and Dr F. R. Leavis in particular, who many years ago helped me to a better understanding of Mr Eliot's work. I hope they will accept this expression of gratitude in place of specific acknowledgments of agreement or disagreement. The critic to whom I owe most, however, is Mr Eliot himself, whose criticism I have drawn on largely to interpret his poetry, and have had in mind even where no direct quotation is made. I have to thank Mr Eliot and Messrs Faber and Faber Ltd for permission to quote from his poetry and prose.

I should like to express my gratitude to Dr Janet Spens for stimulus and encouragement, and to Mrs Duncan-Jones of the University of Birmingham for discussions going back over many years, and particularly for helping me towards an understanding of *Ash Wednesday*. My greatest debt is to Mr John Hayward who first suggested I should write this book and has been most generous in his assistance in both large and small matters.

HELEN GARDNER

St. Hilda's College,
Oxford.

CONTENTS

CHAPTER I

AUDITORY IMAGINATION

'I dare commend him to all that know him as . . . the *Atlas* of Poetrie, and *primus verborum Artifex*.' NASHE on PEELE.

MR ELIOT'S first volume of poems was published more than thirty years ago, and he has by now created the taste by which he is enjoyed. His poetry is no longer the private possession of a small enthusiastic circle of admirers, but is read, as he himself says poets naturally wish to be read, by a 'large and miscellaneous audience'. This audience, though often baffled by difficulties in his thought and manner, as is apparent from the eagerness with which it buys books expounding the poems, has no doubt of his poetic greatness, and feels a real desire to understand more fully both what he says and why he says it in the way he does. Although among older readers there lingers still a certain irritation at what is called his 'obscurity', and although in more sophisticated circles there are signs of the expected revolt against an established reputation, among the young of both sexes, with whom poetry is a passion, there is an unquestioned recognition of his poetic authority and of the profound importance of his poetry.

The study of a poet's art normally begins at the beginning of his career. I am following another method and intend to begin and end with *Four Quartets*. Partly this is because the earlier poetry has been very fully studied by critics such as Professor Matthiessen and Dr Leavis, to whose work I could add little of value, and partly it is because Mr Eliot has reached his widest public with *Four Quartets*. Since this book is largely written for that miscellaneous public it seemed best to begin where many of them had begun. But there is another more important reason. I believe *Four Quartets* is Mr Eliot's masterpiece, and that it contains more fully than any of his earlier works the poetic solution of his peculiar problems as a poet, problems which arise partly from his own temperament, and partly from the conditions under which he has had to write. I shall therefore begin by considering *Four Quartets* as a work of art, and after that I shall attempt to trace the development of his art from the beginning, and to demonstrate the fundamental unity of all his work. The danger of this critical approach is that we should read the later poetry into the earlier, and appear to suggest that the transformation of experience which gives us *Four Quartets* makes in some way invalid the earlier experience which gave us *The Waste Land*. I can only say that I am aware of the danger and have tried to guard against it, and that I do not mean to suggest any inadequacy of poetic expression in the earlier poetry. At every stage Mr Eliot appears to me to have expressed as fully as possible as much as he could express at that stage. But in *Four Quartets* a more richly complex experience finds richer and more varied expression; the range of feeling and the range of the instrument is greater than before. Certain limitations of temperament in the earlier poetry, revealing themselves in certain limitations of imagery and style, are transcended, and there is a complete expression of the subject through the chosen form, which is lacking in the dramas. In this poem, for the four poems must be regarded as essentially one long poem, his art appears at its most daring and assured.

Four Quartets is the mature achievement of a poet who has in a long period of experiment effected a modification and an enrichment of the whole English poetic tradition. It is impossible to believe that poets a hundred years hence will not be aware of what Mr Eliot has done with the English language. They may be developing his way of writing, or they may be reacting against it, they will, one feels certain, be conscious of his poetry as part of their poetic inheritance. Such a modification works backwards as well as forwards. His poetry, in becoming part of English literature, has modified our reading of earlier poetry. We, who have grown up with it, find that we read earlier poetry to some extent through it. It has affected our taste and judgment, by awakening responses to what we might otherwise not have noticed, and by attuning our ears to particular poetic effects and rhythms. Most important of all, it has made us more critically alert to the language of poets. By refreshing the poetic vocabulary of our own day, Mr Eliot has refreshed our appreciation of the poetic diction of earlier poets. He has made us more aware of its different vigour, by making us conscious of the potentialities of the language which we make dull by our common use.

The difference between poets which makes us call one poet a major poet, and deny the title to another, even though we may think him a very good poet, is, I think, after we have made certain other stipulations, a question of the use of language. The major poet's work must have bulk; he must attempt with success one or other of the greater poetic forms, which tests his gifts of invention and variation; he cannot claim the title on a handful of lyrics however exquisite. His subject-matter must have universally recognized importance, and he must treat it with that imaginative authority we call originality; he must have something at once personal and of general relevance to say on important aspects of human experience. These seem to me to be true criteria, if we allow for length and bulk being relative terms, and if we are willing to accept the possibility of new poetic forms. But the further quality which distinguishes the major poet

is a special power of language, a special feeling for the connections of words in sound and meaning. This leads him to
create an idiom and a rhythm that are new and individual,
but which become classic. The major poet is, most of all,
the poet without whose work later poets would not have
written as they did. Such poets not only write poems that are
felicitous in phrase and rhythm, in which the diction seems
exquisitely appropriate, but they revive the very stuff of
poetry, the language and speech-rhythms of their day and
country; they re-create the instrument they use, and suggest
to their contemporaries and to those who come after them
new capacities in the language and new possibilities of
poetic expression. They are those who can

Donner un sens plus pur aux mots de la tribu;

or in Mr Eliot's rendering of Mallarmé's line:

Purify the dialect of the tribe.

The difference is made clear if we think of two great
poets who were contemporaries, such as Chaucer and Langland. Chaucer might well be called a less profoundly serious
poet than Langland; his pathos seems sometimes facile
beside Langland's compassion; his piety conventional beside
Langland's depth of Christian feeling, and intense awareness
of the eternal within the temporal; his irony and humour
can be matched in Langland, and if Langland does not display human diversity so richly, it could be argued that he
makes up for narrowness of range by greater depth of understanding. It could be maintained that Langland was a greater
poet than Chaucer, if our criterion of greatness in a poet
were imaginative vision alone. But Chaucer's 'divine fluid-
ity', his achievement in creating the English heroic line,
wedding the noble verse-forms of Italy to the rhythms of
English speech, his unerring sense of verbal melody, his
skill in the verse paragraph, the range of his vocabulary and

his discretion in the use of it, employing the homely and the exotic in close juxtaposition, the union in his poetry of grace and strength—all these make him a poet who has in a high degree what Langland lacks: what Mr Eliot has called 'auditory imagination'.

The distinction is not the same as the distinction between poets who attempt to bring the language of poetry nearer to common speech, and those who attempt to create for poetry a more elaborate diction and a less colloquial syntax. Auditory imagination may show itself in either way. Donne with all his great gifts almost wholly lacks it. He is as deliberately insensitive to the overtones of words as he is to the associations of ideas and images; in his use of words, as in his use of images, it is not these connections he is seeking. This is not one of the things for which he is 'the first poet in the world'. Spenser, on the other hand, though capable of great flatness and a total lack of verbal distinction for long passages, can at times, and sometimes throughout a whole poem, as in the *Epithalamium*, show this delighted mastery of a rich and varied speech, this power to give words a special life by their context. Like Chaucer he is the creator of a new music. *The Shepheardes Calender* inaugurates an age, where Donne sets a fashion. This is the quality by which Dryden excels Pope, though in almost all other things he is less interesting and delightful. Pope has a far finer sensibility, a far more interesting personality, and his subject-matter, in spite of its apparent limitations, is in fact less ephemeral; he sees deeper into the human heart in his picture of man the social creature, than Dryden does in his picture of man the political creature; he has far more sense of the irony of human fate. Yet great artist as Pope is, he has not the peculiar strength and audacity that Dryden shows in his use of language, just as he has not Dryden's metrical virtuosity. Pope uses the right word; Dryden's rightness is unexpected. He seems to compel words to serve his particular purpose while respecting their general meaning; just as he subordinates speech rhythm to metrical pattern, while leaving the speech rhythm all the time alive and springy within the pattern. Pope seems exact and delicate rather than bold and imaginative in his choice of words, using to perfection the language of his time, but restricting rather than enlarging poetic expression; whereas Dryden continually surprises and delights by a linguistic daring of which 'the first effect is sudden astonishment, the second rational admiration'. It is by virtue of this 'auditory imagination' that Shakespeare excels all other English poets. What Logan Pearsall Smith called 'the enchanted radiance' of his language is achieved by an inventiveness and daring without parallel. He plays in the great ocean of words as buoyantly as Cleopatra's dolphins.

This 'auditory imagination' Mr Eliot has tried to define in prose, and he has further described it in verse. In *The Use of Poetry* (1933), where he used the phrase, he says it is

> the feeling for syllable and rhythm, penetrating far below the conscious levels of thought and feeling, invigorating every word; sinking to the most primitive and forgotten, returning to the origin and bringing something back, seeking the beginning and the end. It works through meanings, certainly, or not without meanings in the ordinary sense, and fuses the old and obliterated and the trite, the current, and the new and surprising, the most ancient and the most civilized mentality.

With the exception of *The Dry Salvages*, each of the Quartets opens its final movement with a consideration of words. Because the poems differ from each other in their moods and in their approach to the common theme, the approach to the mystery of language is different in all three. In *Burnt Norton*, the most abstract and philosophical of the poems, the approach is philosophic and the nature of words is considered:

6

Words move, music moves
Only in time; but that which is only living
Can only die. Words, after speech, reach
Into the silence. Only by the form, the pattern,
Can words or music reach
The stillness, as a Chinese jar still
Moves perpetually in its stillness.
Not the stillness of the violin, while the note lasts,
Not that only, but the co-existence,
Or say that the end precedes the beginning,
And the end and the beginning were always there
Before the beginning and after the end.
And all is always now. Words strain,
Crack and sometimes break, under the burden,
Under the tension, slip, slide, perish,
Decay with imprecision, will not stay in place,
Will not stay still. Shrieking voices
Scolding, mocking, or merely chattering,
Always assail them. The Word in the desert
Is most attacked by voices of temptation,
The crying shadow in the funeral dance,
The loud lament of the disconsolate chimera.

The word itself, like the note in music, has meaning only in relation to other words. It exists in time and in usage; and since contexts and usages change, the life of a word is a continual death. Yet within a pattern, in a poem, the word's life is preserved almost miraculously by art, in a kind of true life beyond its life in speech; it is there stable, not in itself, but in its relations to all the other words in the poem, which in turn are held to their meaning by their relations to it. In *East Coker*, the most tragic in mood and the most personal of the Quartets, the approach is practical; the poet, the craftsman in words, is speaking, not the philosopher. The stress is here on the poet's inevitable defeat, and on the unpropitious circumstances of our own day:

So here I am, in the middle way, having had twenty years—
Twenty years largely wasted, the years of *l'entre deux guerres*—

7

Trying to learn to use words, and every attempt
Is a wholly new start, and a different kind of failure
Because one has only learnt to get the better of words
For the thing one no longer has to say, or the way in which
One is no longer disposed to say it. And so each venture
Is a new beginning, a raid on the inarticulate
With shabby equipment always deteriorating
In the general mess of imprecision of feeling,
Undisciplined squads of emotion. And what there is to conquer
By strength and submission, has already been discovered
Once or twice, or several times, by men whom one cannot hope
To emulate—but there is no competition—
There is only the fight to recover what has been lost
And found and lost again and again: and now, under conditions
That seem unpropitious.

Our age, with its undigested technical vocabulary, its misuse of metaphor,[1] and its servitude to cliché, cannot be regarded as propitious for a poet. It is part of Mr Eliot's greatness as a poet that he has accepted for poetic transformation the idiom of his own day. He has done so deliberately, for he has said:

I believe that any language, so long as it remains the same language, imposes its laws and restrictions and permits its own licence, dictates its own speech rhythms and sound patterns. And a language is always changing; its developments in vocabulary, in syntax, pronunciation and intonation—even, in the long run, its deterioration—must be accepted by the poet and made the best of. He in turn has the privilege of contributing to the development and maintaining the quality, the capacity of the language to express a wide range, and subtle gradation, of feeling and emotion; his task is both to respond to change and make it conscious, and to battle against degradation below the standards which he has learnt from the past (*The Music of Poetry* 1942).

In *East Coker* the poet is thought of as perpetually out-growing his own newly discovered idiom and rhythm. The

[1] It is odd that nobody seems to have asked the Prime Minister, who in 1948 decided to exhort the nation on a thousand hoardings to 'that extra ten per cent of effort that will turn the tide', whether he had ever heard of Canute. The public receives this and similar absurdities about 'targets' and 'ceilings' with absolute calm.

material of his art is itself unstable, and it is at the mercy of feelings that resist the discipline of expression, or make the expression inadequate by their own development beyond what has been expressed. But in *Little Gidding*, in the last tranquil and beautiful movement, the mysterious union of words in poetry, to create a poem, is thought of as a symbol, or rather another manifestation, of the process by which past and future are woven together into meaning in our personal lives and in history. The word and the moment are both points at which meaning is apprehended. The dance of poetry and the dance of life obey the same laws and disclose the same truth:

> What we call the beginning is often the end
> And to make an end is to make a beginning.
> The end is where we start from. And every phrase
> And sentence that is right (where every word is at home,
> Taking its place to support the others,
> The word neither diffident nor ostentatious,
> An easy commerce of the old and the new,
> The common word exact without vulgarity,
> The formal word precise but not pedantic,
> The complete consort dancing together)
> Every phrase and every sentence is an end and a beginning,
> Every poem an epitaph. And any action
> Is a step to the block, to the fire, down the sea's throat
> Or to an illegible stone: and that is where we start.
> We die with the dying:
> See, they depart, and we go with them.
> We are born with the dead:
> See, they return, and bring us with them.
> The moment of the rose and the moment of the yew-tree
> Are of equal duration. A people without history
> Is not redeemed from time, for history is a pattern
> Of timeless moments.

The inevitable defeat of the poet is seen here as the very condition of his existence; and the 'intolerable wrestle with words and meanings' is a type of the exploration which continually brings us back to the place where we started, to begin all over again. The words in parenthesis, expanding the poet's sense of rightness in phrase or sentence, suggesting how it is that words through pattern may 'reach the stillness', describe with the precision of poetry, by themselves illustrating the definition, what is meant by 'auditory imagination'.

These passages from the fifth movements have their part in the music of the whole poem; their poetic rightness is not apparent in isolation, because they depend on what has gone before. To illustrate Mr Eliot's mastery of language one would turn particularly to the first movements, in which the experience on which the rest of the poem is to build its variations is given expression. They can be considered therefore with some propriety by themselves. The first movement of *The Dry Salvages* is particularly beautiful and bold in its diction, its variations of phrasing, and its rhythms. It shows as well as any passage of comparable length the music of his poetry, and provides a convenient starting point for an attempt to define some of the elements in his mature style.

The first paragraph presents in its diction a mingling of the romantic and prosaic, both replaced at the close by another way of speech:

I do not know much about gods; but I think that the river
Is a strong brown god—sullen, untamed and intractable,
Patient to some degree, at first recognized as a frontier;
Useful, untrustworthy, as a conveyor of commerce;
Then only a problem confronting the builder of bridges.
The problem once solved, the brown god is almost forgotten
By the dwellers in cities—ever, however, implacable,
Keeping his seasons and rages, destroyer, reminder
Of what men choose to forget. Unhonoured, unpropitiated
By worshippers of the machine, but waiting, watching and
    waiting.
His rhythm was present in the nursery bedroom,
In the rank ailanthus of the April dooryard,

> In the smell of grapes on the autumn table,
> And the evening circle in the winter gaslight.

The opening line is tentative and colloquial, very different from the firm statement with which *Little Gidding* begins:

> Midwinter spring is its own season
> Sempiternal though sodden towards sundown.

The personification of the river as 'a strong brown god' is a personification which the poet's tone makes no more than a suggestion, a piece of only half-serious myth-making. Words and phrases which are appropriate to a nature god alternate with phrases from common speech, which express a matter-of-fact view. At the beginning vague, emotional adjectives are piled up: 'sullen, untamed and intractable', which are followed by the very different adjectives: 'useful, untrustworthy', words with no emotional tone. And the practical phrases: 'a conveyor of commerce', or 'a problem confronting the builder of bridges', are contrasted with the splendid

>   ever, however, implacable,
> Keeping his seasons and rages, destroyer, reminder
> Of what men choose to forget. Unhonoured, unpropitiated.

These contrasted elements in the diction are fused by a common rhythm in the phrases, so that the flat 'conveyor of commerce' and 'builder of bridges' are given a certain dignity, which they have not got in common speech, by their assimilation to the archaic, almost Biblical, 'dwellers in cities'. This rescues from banality what would in another context be newspaper cliché, the phrase 'worshippers of the machine', and restores its full force of meaning. The different elements in the diction present the contrast between man feeling at the mercy of his environment, which he regards with awe, and man mastering his environment, which he regards with calculation. But at the close of the paragraph the rhythm, which had been relaxed, becomes taut and firm; the general and abstract terms of primitive man worshipping his gods, or civilized man solving his problems, are replaced by precise images: 'the rank ailanthus of the April dooryard', 'the smell of grapes on the autumn table', and 'the evening circle in the winter gaslight'. The words here are exact, not coloured by emotion or lack of emotion; they define particular moments. The emotion is concentrated in the images, so briefly noted. The particular tree, the natural and easy use of the Americanism 'dooryard', and the old-fashioned 'gaslight' fix the images in the poet's childhood. It is in our childish recognition of the changing seasons that we first apprehend the passage of time in our pulses. The imaginative conception of the river as a god biding his time, the ironic conception of the river as something man can use or ignore at will are both discarded. In the first paragraph, in its diction and rhythms, the poet moves from conceptions about nature, from speculations, to our experience as creatures who find ourselves part of a natural order. The myth of primitive man is allied to the child's instinctive recognitions; here is the truth at the heart of the myth.

At the beginning of the second paragraph, where the poet turns to speak of the sea, the firm rhythm continues, but the language takes on a greater force. This is apparent in the powerful verbs, two of them emphasized by the rhyming of the next stressed word. It is in these verbs that the varying moods of the sea are expressed: the encroaching sea in the verb 'reaches', the sea in its careless power in the verb 'tosses', and the sea placid and serene in the verb 'offers':

> The river is within us, the sea is all about us;
> The sea is the land's edge also, the granite
> Into which it reaches, the beaches where it tosses

Its hints of earlier and other creation:
The starfish, the hermit crab, the whale's backbone;
The pools where it offers to our curiosity
The more delicate algae and the sea anemone.
It tosses up our losses, the torn seine,
The shattered lobsterpot, the broken oar
And the gear of foreign dead men. The sea has many voices,
Many gods and many voices.
                                                      The salt is on the briar rose,
The fog is in the fir trees.

The power of this description of the variety of the sea
derives from the variety of the diction. In achieving precision the poetry accommodates the commonplace 'lobsterpot', the technical word 'seine', the botanical 'algae'. The
mysterious phrase 'its hints of earlier and other creation' is
made exact and terrifying by the list of bizarre objects
found upon the beach. The particularity of 'the shattered
lobsterpot' and the 'torn seine' contrasts with the general
word 'gear' in the phrase 'the gear of foreign dead men',
which has an awkward pathos of its own, different from the
pathos of familiar objects broken. This vividly visual passage
is summed up by a return to mythical expression, and by two
images of smell or taste, immediate and pervasive, haunting and formless, images which suggest the eerie menace of
the sea felt inland.

The return to the mythological and these two images of
indefinable sensation introduce the last paragraph, where the
effect is not visual but aural. There are no vigorous verbs
until the close of the movement, where the single verb, long
prepared for and expected, holds our ears, with its single
object.

                              The sea howl
And the sea yelp, are different voices
Often together heard: the whine in the rigging,
The menace and caress of wave that breaks on water,
The distant rote in the granite teeth,

And the wailing warning from the approaching headland
Are all sea voices, and the heaving groaner
Rounded homewards, and the seagull:
And under the oppression of the silent fog
The tolling bell
Measures time not our time, rung by the unhurried
Ground swell, a time
Older than the time of chronometers, older
Than time counted by anxious worried women
Lying awake, calculating the future,
Trying to unweave, unwind, unravel
And piece together the past and the future,
Between midnight and dawn, when the past is all deception,
The future futureless, before the morning watch
When time stops and time is never ending;
And the ground swell, that is and was from the beginning,
Clangs
The bell.

The 'many voices' of the sea, so delicately yet firmly distinguished: the howl, the yelp, the 'whine in the rigging' and 'the menace and caress of wave that breaks on water', almost lull us by the accumulation of experiences and by the regularity of the rhythm, until the expectation of the ear receives a shock in the last sound:

And under the oppression of the silent fog
The tolling bell.

The check in the rhythm brings a change of tone and diction. The contrasts of the opening paragraph return. The majestic conception of the time that is not our time, given grandeur and significance by the liturgical phrase 'that is and was from the beginning', and expressing itself in the final reverberating word 'clangs', contrasts with the time of our daily experience, the time we try to measure exactly by our instruments, the time we try to make sense of in our minds. The commonplace 'anxious worried women', the weakly repetitive verbs 'trying to unweave, unwind, unravel', which, with the following line, 'and piece together the past and the future', suggest an endless process of 'making do and mending', are expressive of a futility which rises to a kind of bleak despair, which has a grandeur of its own in the lines:

> Between midnight and dawn, when the past is all deception,
> The future futureless, before the morning watch
> When time stops and time is never ending.

The words 'before the morning watch' prepare the ear for the final words from the doxology. They are a true point of intersection, bringing together the seaman's watch and the cry of the Psalmist: 'My soul fleeth unto the Lord: before the morning watch, I say, before the morning watch.' Into the desolate silence of the sleepless there breaks the single sound with which the movement ends.

Any attempt such as this to analyse the diction of a passage must murder to dissect, for the life of the passage is in its rhythm, uniting the disparate elements of the diction, and creating, above the varied poetic effects of separate lines and phrases, a single poetic impression. The variety of the diction, the union of the common word and the formal, the colloquial and the remote, the precise and the suggestive, is made possible by the strength and flexibility of the metre —the characteristic metre of *Four Quartets*. The creation of this metre is perhaps Mr Eliot's greatest poetic achievement.

Mr Eliot was from the first a poet with a remarkable range of diction, and with a natural gift for the vividly memorable phrase. He was always consciously aware of the varied resources of English poetic diction and delighted to place an exotic word exactly, or to give us the sudden shock which the unexpected introduction of a commonplace word or phrase can provide. The development in his mature poetry is a development in naturalness: a more 'easy commerce of the old and the new'; a mastery of transitions on the large and the small scale, so that change and variety now 'give delight and hurt not'; and a capacity to employ without embarrassment the obviously poetic word and image. In his earlier poetry he showed a certain distaste for words with poetic associations, which suggested a limitation in his temperament and a certain lack of confidence in his art. Avoidance of the obvious is not the mark of the highest originality or of the genuinely bold artist. The change in Mr Eliot's poetic style which begins with *The Hollow Men* in 1925 is accompanied by a change in his metric. The change in the metre is possibly the fundamental change, for it is the new metre that has made possible his new freedom with the language of poetry.

If we put this change as briefly as possible we might say that on the whole up to *The Waste Land* Mr Eliot's verse could be 'scanned' with as much or as little propriety as most English post-Spenserian verse can be. After *The Hollow Men* this is not so. In this matter of metre the poets go before and the prosodists follow after, often a very long time after. What 'rules' prosodists of the future will discover that Mr Eliot has in practice obeyed I do not know. If I were to try to formulate any now I should almost certainly be proved wrong by whatever verse he writes next. All that someone who is neither a poet nor a prosodist can say at present is that there is a new beginning after *The Waste Land*, which is immediately recognizable, and which is best displayed by the juxtaposition of passages from the earlier and the later poetry. This new beginning is a break with the tradition of English non-lyrical verse, which has been dominant since Spenser displayed in *The Shepheardes Calender* the potentialities of the heroic line.[1]

---

[1] The term 'heroic line' is convenient because it can include the line we find in 'blank verse', in the run-on and heroic forms of the couplet, and in 'heroic stanzas'. Milton employed it to describe his blank verse in the preface to *Paradise Lost*, where he calls it 'English Heroic Verse without Rime'. To call this line an 'iambic pentameter' is seriously misleading. The basis of the

The characteristic metre of *Prufrock and Other Observations* (1917) is an irregularly rhyming verse paragraph in duple rising rhythm, with more or less variation in the length of the lines. Rhyme is used as a rhetorical ornament, not as part of a regular pattern; it is decorative and makes for emphasis, but it is not structural. There is, beside the variety in the number of stresses in the line, considerable variety in the amount of co-incidence between speech stress and metrical stress; but all this we are accustomed to in verse from the seventeenth century onwards. The underlying rhythm is unmistakable; it remains a duple rising rhythm, the staple rhythm of English verse, the basis of our heroic line, whether the line is as short as 'Remark the cat,' or as long as 'But as if a magic lantern threw the nerves in patterns on a screen'. The use of this metre, which is common to 'Prufrock', 'Portrait of a Lady', and, though it is naturally differently handled in the non-dramatic mono- logues, to 'Preludes' and 'Rhapsody on a Windy Night', is an attempt to get away from the dominant blank verse of the nineteenth-century masters of the poetic monologue. Mr

classical iambic line is quantity. Its music arises from the counterpointing of variable speech stresses with a fixed quantitative pattern. The English heroic line has for its base the regular alternation of unstressed(x) and stressed(/) syllables, giving a duple rising rhythm, x /. Its music arises from the counter- pointing of variable speech stresses with regular metrical stresses. Also, while in classical metre the quantitative pattern has actually to be preserved in each line, in English the regular alternation of unstressed and stressed syllables is only an ideal around which the actual line varies. The second fact that makes the use of classical terms improper is that the classical iambic is a light measure. The time is triple, since each foot is made up of a short and a long syllable (a crochet and a minim). The heavy classical metre is the hexameter, which is in duple time. Each foot is either a dactyl (a minim and two crochets), or a spondee (two minims). In English, on the other hand, what used to be called the 'iambic pentameter' is a heavy metre in duple time, our 'heroic' measure. The English 'hexameter' is a light metre, in triple time. The best way, I think, to describe the English heroic line is to say that it is a line of five stresses with an underlying duple rising rhythm. The English 'hexameter', then, is a line of six stresses, with a triple falling rhythm. In read- ing English accentual hexameters we usually fill out the supposed 'spondees' to preserve the tripping waltz time.

Eliot develops instead the free treatment of the heroic line to create paragraphs adorned and pointed by rhyme which we find in poems such as Donne's 'The Apparition', or Herbert's 'The Collar', and in Milton's experiments before he created the blank verse of *Paradise Lost*: 'On Time', 'At a Solemn Music', and, of course, *Lycidas*. What is original is the use to which the metre is put, not the metre itself. Two important poems in the 1917 volume are exceptional. In 'La Figlia Che Piange', though many of the lines if met separately would be identified as common variants of the heroic line, the incantatory repetitions of certain variants, such as the repeated strong stress on the first syllable, take the poem too far from that metrical norm for us to be aware of it as an underlying rhythm; though in the last paragraph we hear it again, in a singularly beautiful handling of this metre. In the other poem, 'Mr Apollinax', the ear discerns no hint of duple rhythm. We have a poem built upon a conversational phrase: a piece of free accentual verse. The speech stress is strong, the pause at the end of the line marked; as it must be for us to feel the pleasure this kind of verse can give, which is the pleasure of catching an emergent rhythm, not that of recognizing an underlying one.

The volume of *Poems* (1920) has abandoned the 'Prufrock' metre. In its place we have the blank verse of 'Gerontion'. The heroic line is handled here with the freedom of the later Elizabethan dramatists. If one can in any sense 'scan' the verse of Tourneur and Middleton, one can scan this. The characteristics of this verse are the extreme freedom in the disposition of the speech stresses, the absence of the strong beat which the co-incidence of speech and metrical stress gives, and the variety in the position of the pauses within the line. This, and other features such as the frequent omission of an initial unstressed syllable and the frequent addition of a final one, is all familiar to us from discussions of the development of Shakespearean and post-Shakespearean blank verse. But magnificent as 'Gerontion' is, there is a flavour in it of *pastiche*. One might call it Mr Eliot's *Hyperion*. We hear his voice through it, but we hear it rather in spite of a voice he is putting on. The majority of the poems in the 1920 volume are in quatrains. This common metre is handled with the greatest brilliance and confidence, reminding us again of the seventeenth century and the wonderful handling of the so-called octosyllabic by the lyric poets of that age. There are all the variations we are accustomed to find: the seven-syllabled and the nine-syllabled lines, the 'trisyllabic feet', but what delights us, as in Donne's 'The Fever', or Marvell's 'A Definition of Love' or Rochester's 'Absent from thee I languish still',[1] is the firmness of the duple rising rhythm, with its strongly marked beat, and the emphatic rhyme. The originality again is not in the metre or in the handling of it, but in the use to which it is put.

The Waste Land (1922) represents the culmination of this period of metrical virtuosity. Its basic measure is the heroic line, which it handles in almost every possible way. One could indeed give a demonstration of the varied music of which this line is capable from *The Waste Land* alone, giving parallels from the work of the most astonishingly diverse poets. We hear the voice of the Jacobean dramatists again in the voice of the thunder at the close. The Shakespearean echoes, apart from direct adaptation, are everywhere. The narrative sweetness of run-on rhyming verse is cruelly caught in

---

[1] I refer to these particular poems because of their masculine vigour. Although they employ two rhymes to the quatrain, where Mr Eliot has only one, this seems less important than the similarity in the run of the verse and the finality of each stanza. The attempt in 'Burbank' to avoid stanzaic finality does not seem to me successful. I feel it to be a failure in metrical taste.

> But at my back from time to time I hear
> The sound of horns and motors, which shall bring
> Sweeney to Mrs Porter in the spring;[1]

and the strength of the end-stopped line gives ironic dignity
to the carbuncular young man's encounter with the typist,
with its regular alternate rhymes. On the other hand, the
beautiful and justly famous opening lines, and the equally
beautiful opening lines of the final section have another
rhythm, not the prevailing duple rising rhythm, but the
repeated falling cadences of 'La Figlia Che Piange'; and the
speech of Lou in the second section, like 'Mr Apollinax',
has escaped entirely from the characteristic rhythm of English
dramatic or quasi-dramatic verse. The voice of the 'poetry
reciter' could make nothing of this.

It may be asked why, if Mr Eliot could do all these
different things with the heroic line, he felt it necessary to
abandon it as the staple metre of his verse. The answer may
be partly given by quoting his adaptation of a line from a
Shakespearean sonnet at the opening of *Ash Wednesday*:

> Because I do not hope to turn again
> Because I do not hope
> Because I do not hope to turn
> Desiring this man's gift and that man's scope. . . .

One meaning of this, if not the principal one, is that from
now on he will try to speak in his own voice, which will
express himself with all his limitations, and not try to escape
those limitations by imitating other poets. The heroic line
is a hindrance in this attempt, because it has so long and
glorious a history that when it is used as the metre of a long
poem it is almost impossible not to echo one or other of its

---

[1] I find it difficult to forgive the outrage committed on Marvell's line, even
though it does illustrate well that the 'heroic line' when used in this way often
takes ten syllables to say what could be better said in eight. The fondness of
the seventeenth century for the 'octosyllabic' is a reaction against the diffuseness of much earlier writing in the 'decasyllabic'.

great masters. Mr Eliot's attack on the 'Chinese Wall' of Milton's verse has only popularized what others have felt and said in the last seventy years or so: the period after the work of Tennyson and Browning, the last poets to show any originality in blank verse. Hopkins's 'sprung rhythm' and Bridges's 'loose alexandrines' in *The Testament of Beauty* are different reactions, the one fertile in influence, the other sterile, to the situation described by Bridges in a review in *The Times Literary Supplement* in 1912:[1]

In all art when a great master appears he so exhausts the material at his disposal as to make it impossible for any succeeding artist to be original, unless he can either find new material or invent some new method of handling the old. In painting and music this is almost demonstrable to the uninitiated; in poetry the law may not be so strict, but it still holds; and any one may see that serious rhyme is now exhausted in English verse, or that Milton's blank verse practically ended as an original form with Milton. There are abundant signs that English syllabic verse has long been in the stage of artistic exhaustion of form which follows great artistic effort. Now as far as regards the verse-form, Wordsworth was apparently unconscious of this predicament. It never occurred to him that he was working with blunted tools. His idea was to purify the diction and revivify English poetry by putting a new content into the old verse forms; and two reasons may be given for this conservatism. First, that in his time an artificial school of poetry had separated itself off from this older tradition, so that any return to the older style appeared to be a freshness; and secondly, he was part of that unaccountable flood of inspiration which in Keats and Shelley and in a few of Coleridge's lyrics transcended in some vital qualities whatever had been done before, and actually wrought miracles of original beauty within the old forms; but these bond-breaking efforts, we should say, more than completed the exhaustion, while the tedious quality of much of their work shows under what hampering conditions the genius of these poets attained excellence. Keats speaks very plainly; he says, for instance, that he relinquished *Hyperion* because he could not get away from Milton; and Mr Synge though he wrote but

[1] See *Collected Essays and Papers*, vol II, No. 13. I owe my knowledge of this to Professor F. P. Wilson, who cited Bridges' comment on the artistic exhaustion of syllabic verse in his book *Elizabethan and Jacobean*.

little verse, seems to have been fully conscious of the poetic situation; indeed he thought it so desperate as to question whether 'before verse can be human again it must not learn to be brutal'.

Up to *The Waste Land* Mr Eliot is on the whole doing what Bridges says the Romantics did: trying to put new content into old forms, and to revive the forms by returning to older handlings of them. Bridges's praise of Keats and Shelley as having 'wrought miracles of original beauty in the old forms' can be applied to him as well as to them. But *The Waste Land* revealed to him, whether consciously or unconsciously, where his own 'Chinese Wall' lay. At all its greatest moments we are conscious of the inescapable power over the poet's ear of the rhythms of the dramatic blank verse of Shakespeare and his followers. Milton, who was deeply read in the dramatists and echoes them again and again in his poetry, escaped from dependence on them by creating his own music. When he had done this, by restoring as the basis of his prosody syllabic regularity, the Shakespearean tone becomes one among the other beauties of *Paradise Lost*.[1] Mr Eliot has not, I think, realized how similar his problem was to Milton's. Milton came at the end of the astonishing development of blank verse on the stage. By the time he reached maturity it had reached decadence. His problem, which one understands best, not by reading *Paradise Lost* in which he has solved it, but by reading *Comus* in which as Johnson says 'may very plainly be discerned the dawn or twilight of *Paradise Lost*', was to do something which Shakespeare had not already done better than he could

---

[1] It is with delight that we hear this accent in lines such as

> For never can true reconcilement grow
> Where wounds of deadly hate have pierc'd so deep.

My tutor, Miss Rooke, who taught me as an undergraduate to listen to the movement of verse, produced these lines one night in company, with the expected result: those that did not recognize them as part of Satan's speech on Mount Niphates searched their memories of the earlier plays of Shakespeare.

hope to. In his British Academy lecture (1947) on Milton Mr Eliot does not quite see this because of the too rigid distinction he makes between dramatic and non-dramatic verse. But his coupling of Shakespeare and Milton together, as poets to be escaped from, gives us the truth which his long critical quarrel with Milton has disguised: that Shakespeare was the real obstacle to his discovery of his own voice:

Milton made a great epic impossible for succeeding generations; Shakespeare made a great poetic drama impossible; such a situation is inevitable, and it persists until the language has so altered that there is no danger, because no possibility, of imitation. Anyone who tries to write poetic drama, even today, should know that half his energy must be exhausted in the effort to escape from the constricting toils of Shakespeare: the moment his attention is relaxed, or his mind fatigued, he will lapse into bad Shakespearian verse. For a long time after an epic poet like Milton, or a dramatic poet like Shakespeare, nothing can be done. Yet the effort must be repeatedly made; for we can never know in advance when the moment is approaching at which a new epic, or a new drama, will be possible; and when the moment does draw near it may be that the genius of an individual poet will perform the last mutation of idiom and versification which will bring that new poetry into being.

Mr Eliot's own practice has not supported the distinction he insists on. His experiments in the writing of dramatic verse have in fact led him to the creation of the metre he has employed for non-dramatic purposes in *Four Quartets*; just as Dryden's long apprenticeship to the stage created out of the poet of *Annus Mirabilis* the poet of *Absalom and Achitophel*. The truth of the matter surely is that much of the verse which occurs in a play is not particularly dramatic, and much of the verse in a long poem may be, if the subject demands it, or if the poet chooses this method of varying the tension in his poem. The speech of Ulysses on degree, a piece of philosophic exposition, is not markedly dramatic, nor is the narrative of Ophelia's death by the Queen in

Hamlet. On the other hand much of the debate in Pandemonium is highly dramatic. What could more naturally express the emotion of the moment than Mammon's outburst of blasphemous exasperation:

> This must be our task
> In Heav'n, this our delight; how wearisom
> Eternity so spent in worship paid
> To whom we hate.

The metre that is most 'natural' on the stage, because it can accommodate the greatest variety of speech rhythms is also the metre most 'natural' in the long poem; but such a metre will receive rather different treatment on the stage from the treatment it will receive in the long poem. The treatment on the stage will be, or ought to be, much freer than the treatment in the long poem need be; because a play must keep nearer to speech rhythms and employ a greater variety of them.

I have said that we are aware of the change in *The Hollow Men*, but it is easier to define what the change is by considering the fragments entitled *Sweeney Agonistes*. Here Mr Eliot attempted to discover by practice 'what forms of versification' are possible on the stage, and to 'find a new form of verse which shall be as satisfactory a vehicle for us as blank verse was for the Elizabethans'.[1] *Sweeney*, which appeared in the *Criterion* in October 1926 and January 1927, shows us the new start in its simplest form. It is at once apparent that it is not an attempt to employ a traditional verse form more flexibly, by bringing it nearer to the rhythms of contemporary speech. Mr Eliot has abandoned the method of 'putting new content into the old verse forms' for the opposite method of finding what is the verse form for the new content. *Sweeney* begins with speech, and speech

[1] 'A Dialogue of Dramatic Poetry' (1928), reprinted in *Selected Essays* (1932).

of the most unpromising kind: the speech, clipped, inexpressive and stale, of modern urban society. It is uneducated speech, but has not the vigour of unsophisticated natural speech; it is flavourless and almost meaningless at times. Mr Eliot tries to discover whether by stressing the characteristic rhythms of this speech we arrive at something that can be called verse. Crites, in Dryden's *Essay of Dramatic Poesy*, attacked rhyme on the stage because he said it 'is uncapable of expressing the greatest thoughts naturally and the lowest it cannot with any grace: for what is more unbefitting the majesty of verse, than to call a servant, or bid a door be shut in rhyme?' This puts the problem of dramatic verse in a nutshell.[1] Mr Eliot approaches the problem of how the greatest thoughts can be expressed naturally, that is with the ring of the living voice, by concentrating on the problem of how we may 'call a servant or bid a door be shut'. If we can discover a poetic rhythm in the most commonplace speech, this rhythm may then be capable of refinement and elevation so that it may accommodate the greatest thoughts without losing naturalness. Some might retort that the rhythm of the heroic line is this 'natural rhythm', since so many writers of English prose fall so easily into it. It may have been so once; but it is noticeable that writers such as Dickens who are prone to this trick usually fall into unconscious blank verse in their poetical passages, when they are indulging in fine writing. This rhythm is not at all characteristic of the living speech of Dickens's characters, unless like Dick Swiveller they are in the 'poetical vein'. It is because the rhythm of blank verse is marked as poetical that modern poets have found it unsatisfactory. Possibly there has been a real alteration in

---

[1] The problem is only more acute on the stage than in the long poem, for the author of a long poem cannot be 'expressing the greatest thoughts' all the time; he needs just as much a medium that is capable of expressing, if not the lowest, at least the less exalted, with grace.

speech rhythms since the sixteenth and seventeenth centuries. Certainly the development of prose rhythms suggests there has been. In *Sweeney* Mr Eliot breaks with the rhythm of the heroic line by finding another music which appears here in its crudest form. The ear discovers a line, heavily end-stopped, often sharply divided into two halves, with four strong beats. The number of syllables is of no importance, nor is the disposition of stressed and unstressed syllables. We can have

> I téll you agáin|it dón't applý
> Déath or lífe|or lífe or déath
> Déath is lífe|and lífe is déath;

or we can have

> In a níce líttle, whíte líttle,|sóft líttle, ténder líttle
> Júicy líttle, ríght líttle,|míssionary stéw.

The short lines often demand to be extended by pauses for emphasis, so that the same time is employed as for the full line:

SWARTS: Thése fellows álways get pínched in the énd.

SNOW: Excúse me, they dón't áll get pínched in the énd.
What abóut them bónes on Épsom Héath?
I séen that in the pápers (*pause*)
You séen it in the pápers (*pause*)
They *dón't* áll get pínched in the énd.

DORIS: A wóman rúns a térrible rísk.

SNOW: Lét Mr Swéeney contínue his stóry.

The ear is aware of the time and the beat, and is occasionally gratified by rhyme, but the pleasure comes in the variety of speech rhythms that can be held to this simple base. *Sweeney* goes back to what Mr Eliot has called 'the essential of percussion and rhythm'. In the concluding chapter of *The Use of Poetry* Mr Eliot said: 'Poetry begins, I dare say, with a savage beating a drum in a jungle.' The drum beat of *Sweeney*, which finds a lyric counterpart in the jazz staccato of the chorus songs, is the base on which Mr Eliot has built his new style. In *Sweeney* he is the innovator, returning, as many innovators have to do, to the primitive elements of his art; in *The Family Reunion* and *Four Quartets* he is the developer, exploiting and elaborating the musical possibilities of his metre. If we think of Milton erecting his original music in blank verse on the basis of syllabic regularity, we can think of Mr Eliot, in revolt against this, as Milton revolted against the licence of the dramatists, building his music on an emphatic stress, or beat.

To relate Mr Eliot's 'new verse' to the English poetic tradition, we must go back to Spenser and that manifesto of the 'new poetry' of the sixteenth century, *The Shepheardes Calender*. The main importance of the *Calender* prosodically is that in it Spenser handles the heroic line with the ease, grace and rhythmic freedom which Chaucer, its creator, had displayed, but which had virtually disappeared since Chaucer's death. The exquisite lyrics in the April and November eclogues, in which he shows a similar mastery in rhythmic variation in an elaborate stanza, each verse varying around an ideal pattern, are less significant. Though there had been nothing so elaborately musical before, English lyric verse had not suffered the same degradation as had the heavier metres. The other striking feature of the *Calender* is the accentual metre of February, May and September. This Spenser plainly thought of as a metre of 'pastoral rudeness'. Its employment for these 'wise shepherd' eclogues is part of his 'dewe obseruing of Decorum eueryewhere'. Its nature is at once apparent, though its origins have been much discussed:

CUDDIE

Ah for pittie, wil rancke Winters rage,
These bitter blasts neuer ginne tasswage?
The kene cold blowes through my beaten hyde,
All as I were through the body gryde.
My ragged rontes all shiver and shake,
As doen high Towers in an earthquake:
They wont in the wind wagge their wrigle tailes,
Perke as Peacock: but nowe it auales.

THENOT

Lewdly complainest thou laesie ladde,
Of Winters wracke, for making thee sadde.
Must not the world wend in his commun course
From good to badd, and from badde to worse,
From worse vnto that is worst of all,
And then returne to his former fall?

There is no question here of a regularly rising or falling
rhythm, nor of a regularly occurring duple time. The great
majority of the lines have four beats, though lines with five
beats may occur, and we read by the time and the beat.
Without entering into debate on what Spenser thought he
was doing, we can say that he is in fact trying the experiment
of combining an irregular accentual line with regular rhyme.
The rhyme takes the place of the alliteration which was the
other formal element beside stress in the Middle English
development of the Old English metrical system. He discovered no doubt in the writing, as we do in the reading,
that the apparent freedom of the verse is illusory. It becomes
only a dull thumping noise as one reads on. But his use of
the metre remains an interesting hint of the way English
poetry might have developed, if Spenser had been more
interested in working out a way to achieve genuine freedom
in accentual verse, and had not instead discovered the
excellence of the heroic line. In doing this he inaugurated
three hundred years of English poetry.

Mr Eliot, feeling like Bridges that the form was exhausted,
has been bolder than Bridges was. Bridges attempted a

modification of Milton's syllabic verse. Mr Eliot has gone behind the heroic line to develop the kind of metre that Spenser only toyed with in the *Calender*. Whether he realized it or not when he made the experiment of *Sweeney Agonistes*, he was taking up and remaking for his own purposes, or perhaps we might say finding his way back to, the medieval tradition of accentual verse. Spenser, I think, missed his way because he tried to combine this kind of line with regular rhyme. When Coleridge attempted the same kind of experiment in *Christabel*, his ear taught him that the regularity of the rhyme called for some answering regularity in the metre, and he modified the whole effect by employing a predominantly rising rhythm. The result is a masterpiece of musical beauty, but the metre, beautifully suited to Coleridge's romantic, magic tale, has none of the qualities necessary for a 'maid-of-all-work' metre. The great quality of Mr Eliot's new verse is its rhythmic flexibility. I suspect that the element which prosodists will concentrate on in the future is the use he makes of quantity to counterpoint his stress. But anyone can hear that he employs at will rising or falling rhythms, and that he can fall into the evenness of duple or the ripple of triple rhythm, according to the particular effect he wants.

The norm to which the verse constantly returns is the four-stress line, with strong medial pause, with which *Burnt Norton* opens:

> Time present|and time past
> Are both perhaps present|in time future,
> And time future|contained in time past.[1]

[1] In verse of this kind the reading of certain lines will vary with the individual reader. I am aware that other readers may disagree with some of the stresses I mark, and that at times my emphasis differs slightly from Mr Eliot's own in his recorded readings. I have risked the possibility of arousing disagreement over details in order to make the main points clear.

The ear accepts as perfectly natural the extension to five stresses in the third line; which gives finality to the opening statement, without creating uncertainty of expectation. In the same way the three-stress line

> Footfalls echo in the memory

is extended by a natural speech pause before we come to

> Down the passage|which we did not take
> Towards the door|we never opened.

The emergence of this line, after a preliminary introduction in a variation of it, makes the close of the first paragraph of *The Dry Salvages* so movingly authoritative:

> His rhythm was present|in the nursery bedroom,
> In the rank ailanthus|of the April dooryard,
> In the smell of grapes|on the autumn table,
> And the evening circle|in the winter gaslight.

It emerges also strongly dominant in the first movement of *East Coker* after the beautiful slow introductory paragraph, where there are many lines of five stresses, one of eight, and a concluding one of six:

> Keeping time,
> Keeping the rhythm|in their dancing
> As in their living|in the living seasons
> The time of the seasons|and the constellations
> The time of milking|and the time of harvest
> The time of the coupling|of man and woman
> And that of beasts.|Feet rising and falling.
> Eating and drinking.|Dung and death.

Little Gidding, like *Burnt Norton*, on the other hand, gives out the time in its first line. Here the line, which seems so limited when it opens *Burnt Norton*, reveals at once its capacity for splendour:

> Midwinter spring|is its own season
> Sempiternal|though sodden towards sundown,
> Suspended in time|between pole and tropic.
> When the short day is brightest,|with frost and fire,
> The brief sun flames the ice,|on pond and ditches,
> In windless cold|that is the heart's heat,
> Reflecting in a watery mirror
> A glare that is blindness|in the early afternoon.

If we put this beside the opening of *Piers Plowman* which its combination of alliteration with stress immediately recalls, we can see what is comparable and what is not:

> In a somer seson   whan soft was the sonne,
> I shope me in shroudes   as I a shepe were,
> In habite as an heremite   vnholy of workes,
> Went wyde in this world   wondres to here.
> Ac on a May mornynge   on Maluerne hulles
> Me byfel a ferly   of fairy me thoughte;
> I was wery forwandred   and went me to reste
> Vnder a brode banke   bi a bornes side,
> And as I lay and lened   and loked in the wateres,
> I slombred in a slepyng   it sweyued so merye.

The great defect of Langland's metre is its monotony. There is variety within the line, but the pace is too unvarying. Mr Eliot has freed the metre by exercising a far greater liberty within the line in the number of syllables, and by using the four-stress line as a norm to depart from and return to. This makes the paragraph a rhythmical whole, as it is not in Langland, where we are too conscious of the line as the unit of the verse.

There are two obvious main variations of this metre in *Four Quartets*. There is the shorter line of three stresses with which *Burnt Norton* closes, where the occasional four-stress lines appear as exceptional:

> The detail of the pattern is movement,
> As in the figure of the ten stairs.
> Desire itself is movement
> Not in itself desirable;
> Love is itself unmoving,
> Only the cause and end of movement,
> Timeless, and undesiring
> Except in the aspect of time
> Caught in the form of limitation
> Between un-being and being.
> Sudden in a shaft of sunlight
> Even while the dust moves
> There rises the hidden laughter
> Of children in the foliage
> Quick now, here, now, always
> Ridiculous the waste sad time
> Stretching before and after.

The beautiful variations on this base at the close of each of the other Quartets reveal its possibilities, only hinted at in the passage in *Burnt Norton*, as a medium for the more lyrical moments. It occurs with poignant effect in the scene between Harry and Mary in *The Family Reunion*, where dramatic intercourse yields for a moment to something else:

> Pain is the opposite of joy
> But joy is a kind of pain
> I believe the moment of birth
> Is when we have knowledge of death
> I believe the season of birth
> Is the season of sacrifice
> For the tree and the beast, and the fish
> Thrashing itself upstream:
> And what of the terrified spirit
> Compelled to be reborn
> To rise toward the violent sun
> Wet wings into the rain cloud
> Harefoot over the moon?

The other obvious variation is the long line of six stresses with which the second half of the second movement of *Burnt Norton* opens:

At the still point of the turning world.|Neither flesh nor fleshless;
Neither from nor towards;|at the still point, there the dance is,
But neither arrest nor movement.|And do not call it fixity,
Where past and future are gathered.|Neither movement from
    nor towards,
Neither ascent nor decline.|Except for the point, the still point,
There would be no dance,|and there is only the dance.
I can only say, *there* we have been:|but I cannot say where.
And I cannot say, how long,|for that is to place it in time.

33

The last three lines mark an alteration of the rhythm, by a reduction of the stresses to five, in preparation for a return to the four-stress line which is the base for the remainder of the movement. It concludes emphatically with

> Ónly through time|time is cónquered.

The most magnificent handling of this long line is in the third movement of *East Coker*. The first line sets the time:

> O dárk dárk dárk. They áll go ínto the dárk.

Here again the transformation of the base toward the close of the movement is most masterly and deeply moving. We return at the close once more by means of a passage where the base is five stresses to

> So the dárkness shall be the líght,|and the stíllness the dáncing.
> Whísper of running stréams,|and wínter líghtning.
> The wíld thyme unséen and the wíld stráwberry,
> The láughter in the gárden,|echoed écstasy
> Not lóst, but requíring,|póinting to the ágony
> Of déath and bírth.

The most delightful variation of this six-stress line is at the opening of *The Dry Salvages*, whose first lines

> I dó not know múch about góds;|but I thínk that the ríver
> Is a stróng brown gód—|súllen, untámed and intráctable,

immediately recall the rhythm of the accentual 'hexameter'.[1] One imagines that this rhythm, the rhythm of *Evangeline*,

---

[1] Accentual 'hexameter' lines are very common in speech. Mrs Ing of Lady Margaret Hall, to whom I am greatly indebted for assistance in the discussion of prosody, allows me to quote an example which delighted her once at a dinner-party, where her eye fell on this: 'In perfect condition when bottled, but care should be used in decanting.'

came almost unconsciously here among memories of early childhood. Mr Eliot has never been one to despise a 'good tune'. When he selected a group of poems to be broadcast by the BBC in 1947—not his favourite poems, but poems that stayed in his head and came to his mind at moments when he was thinking of nothing much else—it was noticeable that after Johnson's 'Elegy on Dr Robert Levett', all the poems he chose, with the exception of Shelley's 'Art thou pale for weariness', were 'thumpers': Scott's 'Bonny Dundee', Poe's 'For Annie', Kipling's 'Danny Deever', Davidson's 'Thirty Bob a Week'. And Old Possum, though the name suggests senility and taciturnity, is lusty and uninhibited in the rhythms which enchant young listeners.[1] Not the least of the merits of Mr Eliot's new verse is that it allows him to include within his total musical effect adaptations of these emphatic rhythms, which for most of us were our first introduction to the delight of metrical speech.

The supreme merit of his new verse, however, is the liberty it has given him to include every variety of diction, and to use the poetic as boldly as the prosaic, without any constraint. It has enabled him also to express his own vision of life in a form in which that vision can be perfectly embodied: the Quartet form, which depends on the kind of rhythmic variation which the new verse has made possible.

---

[1] An aversion to cats, as strong as Mr Eliot's confessed antipathy to Milton as a man, compels me to treat Old Possum, as Mr Eliot has treated Milton, as a musician, whose subject-matter is of no interest. The reasons for these aversions we may leave to the psychological critics. The brilliant dexterity of the verse in *Old Possum's Book of Practical Cats* (1939) has hardly been recognized.

CHAPTER II

THE MUSIC OF 'FOUR QUARTETS'

And thou, sweet Music, Dancing's only life,
The ear's sole happiness, the Air's best speech,
Loadstone of fellowship, Charming rod of strife,
The soft mind's Paradise, the sick mind's Leech.

SIR JOHN DAVIES, Orchestra

BY calling his poem *Four Quartets*, Mr Eliot has made it necessary for any critic, even though as ignorant as he confesses himself to be of 'a technical knowledge of musical form', to discuss the debt he owes to the art of music in his solution of the problem of finding a form for the long poem. He has given some indications of what that debt is in his lecture on *The Music of Poetry*.

I think that a poet may gain much from the study of music: how much technical knowledge of musical form is desirable I do not know, for I have not that technical knowledge myself. But I believe that the properties in which music concerns the poet most nearly, are the sense of rhythm and the sense of structure. I think that it might be possible for a poet to work too closely to musical analogies: the result might be an effect of artificiality; but I know that a poem, or a passage of a poem, may tend to realize itself first as a particular rhythm before it reaches expression in words, and that this rhythm may bring to birth the idea and the image; and I do not believe that this is an experience peculiar to myself. The use of recurrent themes is as natural to poetry as to music. There are possibilities for verse which bear some analogy to the development of a theme by different groups of instruments; there are possibilities of transitions in a poem comparable to the different movements of a symphony or a quartet; there are possibilities of contrapuntal arrangement of subject-matter. It is in the concert room, rather than in the opera house, that the germ of a poem may be quickened.

As the title shows, each poem is structurally a poetic

equivalent of the classical symphony, or quartet, or sonata, as distinct from the suite. This structure is clear when all four poems are read, as they are intended to be, together, and is essentially the same as the structure of *The Waste Land*. It is far more rigid than would be suspected from reading any one of the poems separately, but it is sufficiently flexible to allow of various arrangements and modifications of its essential features. It is capable of the symphonic richness of *The Waste Land* or the chamber-music beauty of *Burnt Norton*. The form seems perfectly adapted to its creator's way of thinking and feeling: to his desire to submit to the discipline of strict poetic laws, and at the same time to have liberty in the development of a verse capable of extremes of variation, and in the bringing together of ideas and experiences often divorced. The combination of apparent licence with actual strictness corresponds to the necessities of his temperament.

Each poem contains what are best described as five 'movements', each with its own inner necessary structure. The first movement suggests at once a musical analogy. In each poem it contains statement and counter-statement, or two contrasted but related themes, like the first and second subjects of a movement in strict sonata form. The analogy must not be taken too literally. Mr Eliot is not imitating 'sonata form', and in each poem the treatment or development of the two subjects is slightly different. The simplest is the treatment of the river and sea images in *The Dry Salvages*, the symbols for two different kinds of time: the time we feel in our pulses, in our personal lives, and the time we become aware of through our imagination, stretching behind us, beyond the record of the historian, and continuing after we have gone. The two subjects are presented successively, in contrast. The first movement of *Burnt Norton* shows a similar division into two statements. Here the contrast is between abstract speculation and an experience in a garden, a meditation on consciousness and a presentation of consciousness. But in *East Coker* the first movement falls into four parts. The first theme of the time of the years and the seasons, the rhythm of birth, growth and death, is resumed in the third paragraph, and the second theme, the experience of being outside time, of time having stopped, is briefly restated at the close. While in *Little Gidding*, the most brilliantly musical of the four poems, the third paragraph is a development of the first two, weaving together phrases taken up from both in a kind of counterpointing. In general, however, it is true to say that the first movement is built on contradictions which the poem is to reconcile.

The second movement is constructed on the opposite principle of a single subject handled in two boldly contrasted ways. The effect is like that of hearing the same melody played on a different group of instruments, or differently harmonized, or hearing it syncopated, or elaborated in variations, which cannot disguise the fact that it is the same. The movement opens with a highly poetical lyric passage, in a traditional metrical form: irregularly rhyming octosyllabics in *Burnt Norton* and *East Coker*, a simplified sestina[1] in *The Dry Salvages* and three lyric stanzas in *Little Gidding*. This is followed immediately by an extremely colloquial passage, in which the idea which had been treated in metaphor and symbol in the first half of the movement is expanded and developed in a conversational manner. In the

[1] The *sestina* is a poem of six six-line stanzas, each stanza repeating the rhyme words of the first but re-arranging them. There is often a coda of three lines with the rhyme words in their original order in the middle and end of each line. Spenser adopted a simpler form of re-arrangement of the rhymes than the Italian *sestina* shows in his August Eclogue, no doubt to suit our duller ears. Mr Eliot does not re-arrange his rhymes, as he wishes to give the effect of repetition without progression, a wave-like rise and fall. He also does not confine himself to the repetition of the six rhyme words of the first stanza, employing other rhymes and sometimes assonance, and only returning to the original rhyme words in his last stanza.

first three poems the metre used is the same as the metre of the first movement, though in each case here the passage begins with the long line; in *Little Gidding* a modification of *terza rima* is employed. In *Burnt Norton*, the highly obscure, richly symbolic presentation of the 'flux of life' perceived as a unity in the consciousness, turns to a bare statement in philosophic language of the relation of stillness and movement, past, present and future. At the close there is a return to imagery, when after the abstract discussion three concrete moments are mentioned:

> the moment in the rose-garden,
> The moment in the arbour where the rain beat,
> The moment in the draughty church at smokefall.

In *East Coker* we have first a confusion in the seasons and the constellations. This turns to a flat statement of the same confusion in the lives of individual men, where the settled wisdom of old age is dismissed as a deception. Imagery returns here also, in the expansion of Dante's 'selva oscura':

> In the middle, not only in the middle of the way
> But all the way, in a dark wood, in a bramble,
> On the edge of a grimpen, where is no secure foothold,
> And menaced by monsters, fancy lights,
> Risking enchantment.

Again in the last two lines

> The houses are all gone under the sea.

> The dancers are all gone under the hill,

we have a faint recalling of the whole of the first movement, the briefest possible evocation of what was there said. In *The Dry Salvages* the beautiful lament for the anonymous, the endless sum of whose lives adds up to no figure we can name, and leaves little trace but wrecks and wastage on time's ocean, hints in its last stanza where meaning can be found, and the hint is then developed directly, at first with little metaphor, but at the close with a full and splendid return to the original images of the river and the sea. This return to imagery in *The Dry Salvages* comes with wonderful power and force after the purging of our minds by the colloquial and discursive passage in which the poet has deliberately deprived himself of the assistance of imagery. It is a poetic effect comparable to the moment when, after a long and difficult passage of musical development, the original melody returns with all its beauty. The particular treatment of the second movement in *The Dry Salvages* is the poetic expression of its subject:

> We had the experience but missed the meaning,
> And approach to the meaning restores the experience.

The effort to find meaning restores the original imaginative vision of the river and the sea; the images return with power. In *Little Gidding* the exquisite lyric on the decay of our mortal world changes to the colloquy with the 'dead master', after the air-raid, when human fame and the achievement of the poet are likewise shown to be vanity. The second part of the movement, though metrically distinct from the first, is metrically formal[1] and imagery runs through it. This is in keeping with the whole tenor of *Little Gidding* in which the stylistic contrasts are less violent than in the two middle poems and one is more conscious of the counterpointing of themes. As in the first movement then, the relation between the two parts varies with the character of each poem. We can say generally that the first part is traditional in its metre, symbolic, romantic in its imagery, and lyrical; and

[1] The metre is an original modification of *terza rima*. The 'want of like terminations' in an uninflected language such as English involves most translators and imitators of Dante in a loss of his colloquial terseness and austere nobility in an effort to preserve the rhyme. Mr Eliot has sacrificed rhyme, and by substituting for it alternate masculine and feminine endings, he has preserved the essential forward movement of the metre, without loss of directness of speech and naturalness.

the second part discursive, colloquial, meditative. But in
Burnt Norton the second part is philosophic and abstract, in
East Coker and *The Dry Salvages* it is personal and reflective
—more immediately personal in *East Coker* and more
generally reflective in *The Dry Salvages*—and in *Little Gidding* it is particular, and the reflection arises out of a firmly
established situation.

In the third movement one is less conscious of musical
analogies. The third movement is the core of each poem,
out of which reconcilement grows: it is an exploration with
a twist of the ideas of the first two movements. At the close
of these centre movements, particularly in *East Coker* and
Little Gidding, the ear is prepared for the lyric fourth movement. The repetitive circling passage in *East Coker*, in
particular, where we seem to be standing still, waiting for
something to happen, for a rhythm to break out, reminds
one of the bridge passages and leading passages between
two movements which Beethoven loved. The effect of
suspense here is comparable to the sensation with which we
listen to the second movement of Beethoven's Violin Con-
certo finding its way towards the rhythm of the Rondo. But
the organization of the movement itself is not fixed. In
Burnt Norton it falls into two equal parts, divided by a change
of mind, with no change of metre. In *East Coker* the change
of feeling is not represented by a break. The break in the
metre occurs after the change the movement records has
occurred. The change is one that 'comes upon' the mind:
'the darkness shall be the light, and the stillness the dancing'.
There is a change in the rhythm, not a break, from the
six-stress line to the four-stress. Then after a pause there
comes the 'bridge passage', in which we wait for the moment
when its 'requiring' is answered by the firm rhythm of the
great Passion lyric. In *The Dry Salvages* there is no real break;
but there is a change in temper from the reflective to the

hortatory, represented by a similar change of rhythm from the tentative six-stress line to the firm handling of the line of four stresses. In *Little Gidding* there is a very definite break as the poet changes from the personal to the historic. The poet here turns to the beautiful three-stress line which before this was reserved for the close of the last movement.

After the brief lyrical movement, the fifth recapitulates the themes of the poem with personal and topical applications and makes a resolution of the contradictions of the first. It falls into two parts in each poem, but the change is slighter than in the second movement, and it is reversed. Here the colloquial passage comes first, and then, without a feeling of sharp break, for the metre remains fundamentally the same, the base of the line contracts and images return in quick succession. In various ways the last lines echo the beginning of the whole poem or employ images from the other poems in a conclusion of tender gravity, touched at times by a lyric sweetness.

The Waste Land, if one allows for its much wider scope, its essentially dramatic method of presentation, and its hosts of characters, follows the same main pattern. 'The Burial of the Dead' contains far more than two statements, but formally it is a series of contrasts of feeling towards persons and experiences, which are related by a common note of fear. 'The Game of Chess' opens with the elaborate, highly poetic description of the lady at her dressing table, a passage like a set-piece of description in a late Elizabethan play. This contrasts with the talk of Lou and her friends in the public-house at closing time. But the violence of the stylistic contrast only makes clearer the underlying similarity of emotion: boredom and panic, and the common theme of sterility. There is something comparable to the return of images at the close of this section in the Quartets in the use made of Ophelia's words: 'Good night, sweet ladies, good night', though here the effect is ironical. 'The Fire Sermon', the poem's heart, has moments when the oppression lifts, and a feeling of release and purification floods in. This twist is given by the evocations of another world than the appalling world of the twining serpents which Tiresias sees. The reference to the Buddha, the 'collocation of western and eastern asceticism', to which attention is drawn in the notes, anticipates the use of the *Bhagavad-Gita* in the same movement of *The Dry Salvages*. 'Death by Water', the fourth movement, is again a brief lyric, and the fifth section, 'What the Thunder Said', while being naturally far more complex than the final movements of the Quartets, performs the same function of resolution. It returns also to many of the themes of the first movement, recalling its crowds, as well as the separate figures of the second and third movements, and treating again of its theme of birth and death.

It is obvious, however, that, in spite of the basic similarity of structure, the form is far more highly developed in *Four Quartets*, and that both the whole poem and the separate poems depend upon the form in a way that *The Waste Land* does not. In *The Waste Land* Mr Eliot took the Grail myth, as interpreted by Miss Weston, for his ostensible subject, or starting point. *The Waste Land* is given coherence not by its form, but by this underlying myth, to which constant reference can be made, and of which all the varied incidents and the many personages are illustrative. But in *Four Quartets* the title of the whole poem tells us nothing of its subject, and the titles of the separate poems tell us very little. The poems are not 'about places' though their subjects are bound up with particular places.[1] There are no books to

---

[1] When a resident of East Coker, justly enthusiastic over its beauty, said to me: 'Personally, I don't think Eliot has done justice to the village', it was difficult to do anything but agree, without wounding local pride by the suggestion that he had not really tried to.

On the other hand failure to recognize that the titles are place-names may

which we can direct an inquirer. The works of St John of the Cross, though relevant, will not help a reader in the same way as *The Golden Bough* or *From Ritual to Romance* will in Mr Eliot's own words 'elucidate the difficulties' of *The Waste Land*. We might begin a description of *Four Quartets* by saying it presents a series of meditations upon existence in time, which, beginning from a place and a point in time, and coming back to another place and another point, attempts to discover in these points and places what is the meaning and content of an experience, what leads to it, and what follows from it, what we bring to it and what it brings to us. But any such description will be brief and abstract; we have to use words like 'time', 'memory', 'consciousness', words whose meaning we do not really grasp, abstractions from sensation. We shall find we are leaving out all that makes the poem memorable, whereas if we told the story of the Fisher King we should be leading a reader towards the poetry of *The Waste Land*. It is better to abandon these abstractions and return to a consideration of the form, to which the meditation owes its coherence. The form is inspired by the composer's power to explore and define, by continual departures from, and returns to, very simple thematic material. The 'thematic material' of the poem is not an idea or a myth, but partly certain common symbols. The basic symbols are the four elements, taken as the material of mortal life, and another way of describing *Four Quartets* and a less misleading one, would be to say that *Burnt Norton* is a poem about air, on which whispers are borne,

mislead. 'Je suppose que le quatrième quatuor, *Little Gidding*, porte le nom d'un petit garçon cher à T. S. Eliot,' writes a Belgian critic, Pierre Messiaen (*Etudes*, décembre 1948). But his summary of the poem's 'message' does not suggest that a mere understanding of the title would have helped him very much: 'A ce petit garçon, l'auteur veut léguer trois pensées: que la vie est dure, qu'elle est composée d'echecs et qu'elle est sans cesse un recommencement. Ce qui compte, c'est que le feu brûle et la rose fleurisse.'

intangible itself, but the medium of communication;[1] *East Coker* is a poem about earth, the dust of which we are made and into which we shall return; it tells of 'dung and death', and the sickness of the flesh; *The Dry Salvages* is a poem about water, which some Greek thinkers thought was the primitive material out of which the world arose, and which man has always thought of as surrounding and embracing the land, limiting the land and encroaching on it, itself illimitable;[2] *Little Gidding* is a poem about fire, the purest of the elements, by which some have thought the world would end, fire which consumes and purifies. We could then say that the whole poem is about the four elements whose mysterious union makes life, pointing out that in each of the separate poems all four are present; and perhaps adding that some have thought that there is a fifth element, unnamed but latent in all things: the quintessence, the true principle of life, and that this unnamed principle is the subject of the whole poem.

By relying on form and these simple underlying symbols, Mr Eliot has found not only a personal solution of his personal problems as a poet, but a solution, which may greatly influence later writers, of the problem of the long poem. He has freed it from its dependence on a subject that can be expressed in non-poetic terms. In lyric poetry, particularly in brief lyrics and songs, it is often true to say that the subject cannot be separated from the poem; but the longer meditative poem has usually to find a subject which is

---

[1] Donne speaks of air in this way, as a necessary medium, in 'The Extasie':

> On man heavens influence workes not so,
> But that it first imprints the ayre.

In Sir John Davies's *Orchestra*, in the passage from which I have taken the epigraph for this chapter, there is a disquisition on Air also:

> For what are breath, speech, echoes, music, winds
> But Dancings of the Air, in sundry kinds?

[2] A glance at a collection of early maps shows how man instinctively conceives the sea as 'the land's edge'.

separable from the poetry, though often of little interest in itself when so separated. One can, for instance, 'summarize the argument' of the *De Rerum Natura*; one can give a factual account of Wordsworth's life from *The Prelude*; one can 'trace the development of the thought' in *In Memoriam*. But with *Four Quartets* we cannot summarize the argument, nor can we say 'what happens'. Mr Eliot has not given us a poem of philosophic argument, though his poem includes philosophic argument. He would probably assent to Keats's confession: 'I have never yet been able to perceive how anything can be known for truth by consequitive reasoning.' He has not related to us in autobiographical narrative 'the growth of a poet's mind', though this would be one possible sub-title for *Four Quartets*. The difficulty of employing an autobiographical framework is that the present is always ahead. The Red Queen and *Tristram Shandy* both show us how hard one has to run to keep in the same place. The poet who sets out to tell us what brought him 'to this place and hour' has passed on to another place and hour by the time he comes to finish. There cannot be a true conclusion. By rejecting autobiography, Mr Eliot has been able to include without difficulty, and with perfect relevance, experience that was in the future when the poem was planned. The poem has grown with the poet and changed with changing circumstances, without out-growing its original plan. *Burnt Norton* was published in the *Collected Poems* (1936) and it was announced then that it was the first of a series of four Quartets. The scheme appears to have been laid aside while *The Family Reunion* was written. *East Coker* was not published until Good Friday 1940, and came with extraordinary appropriateness. Its words:

And that, to be restored, our sickness must grow worse,

seemed prophetic at that time of waiting, the period of war

that was not war. When *The Dry Salvages* appeared the war
at sea was at its height, and *Little Gidding* includes without
any distortion of its original purpose a fire-raid on London
and a warden's patrol in Kensington. But while *Four
Quartets* shares with a spiritual diary such as *In Memoriam*
the power to include present experience without irrelevance,
it escapes the diary's defect of diffuseness and lack of concentration. The diary can give us a sense of progress and
development, but not the sense of the end implicit in the
beginning, of necessary development; it has the interest of
narrative, not the deeper delight of plot. In the long poem
that depends on the day-to-day development of a mind, the
parts will seem greater than the whole, and even Tennyson's
powers of variation can hardly save *In Memoriam* as a whole
from the monotony of life and give it the coherence of art.
The form of *Four Quartets* transforms living into art, not
thought, gives us a sense of beginning and ending, of the
theme having been fully worked out, which is rare in the
long poem. The separate parts combine in a way that the
sonnets of a sonnet sequence, or a series of repeated stanzas
cannot. The strict limitations of the form make possible
the freedom of the treatment. The poet can say what he
wishes because he must say it in this way. The nearest
analogy I can suggest is the Greek Pindaric Ode, and Mr
Eliot might be said to have succeeded in finding what
earlier English poets had tried to find, a proper English
equivalent for the formal ode. Here again, as in his metrical
experiments, he has found a way suited to the genius of the
English language, which has formed, and been formed by,
the English ear, impatient of the kind of elaborate pattern
that the Greeks and Italians enjoyed. He has not in any sense
imitated the Pindaric Ode, but he has found a kind of
equivalent: an original form supplying the same need, and
giving something of the same delight. The strict Pindaric

has never seemed more than a feat of virtuosity in English, while the loose Pindaric has too little formal organization to give pleasure; it arouses no expectancy, and so cannot delight by satisfying or surprising. The Quartet form, though capable of almost unlimited variations, has a secure formal basis by which we recognize the variations as variations.

The more familiar we become with *Four Quartets*, however, the more we realize that the analogy with music goes much deeper than a comparison of the sections with the movements of a quartet, or than an identification of the four elements as 'thematic material'. One is constantly reminded of music by the treatment of images, which recur with constant modifications, from their context, or from their combination with other recurring images, as a phrase recurs with modifications in music. These recurring images, like the basic symbols, are common, obvious and familiar, when we first meet them. As they recur they alter, as a phrase does when we hear it on a different instrument, or in another key, or when it is blended and combined with another phrase, or in some way turned round, or inverted. A simple example is the phrase 'a shaft of sunlight' at the close of *Burnt Norton*. This image occurs in a rudimentary form in *The Hollow Men*, along with a moving tree and voices heard in the wind:

> There, the eyes are
> Sunlight on a broken column
> There, is a tree swinging
> And voices are
> In the wind's singing
> More distant and more solemn
> Than a fading star.

At the close of *Burnt Norton* a 'moment of happiness', defined in *The Dry Salvages* as a 'sudden illumination' is made concrete by the image of a shaft of sunlight which transfigures the world:

> Sudden in a shaft of sunlight
> Even while the dust moves
> There rises the hidden laughter
> Of children in the foliage
> Quick now, here, now, always—
> Ridiculous the waste sad time
> Stretching before and after.

This is the final concrete statement of what *Burnt Norton* is about; but it recalls the experience we have been given in a different rhythm and with different descriptive accompaniments in the second half of the first movement, as the sun for a moment shines from the cloud, and the whole deserted garden seems to become alive:

> Dry the pool, dry concrete, brown edged,
> And the pool was filled with water out of sunlight,
> And the lotos rose, quietly, quietly,
> The surface glittered out of heart of light,
> And they were behind us, reflected in the pool.
> Then a cloud passed, and the pool was empty.

The image repeated, but with such a difference, at the close establishes the validity of the first experience. Brief and illusory as it appears in the first movement, it has not been dismissed. It has remained in thought and it returns. Thōugh

> Time and the bell have buried the day
> The black cloud carries the sun away,

when the 'sudden shaft' falls, it is time that seems the illusion.

But this image of 'a shaft of sunlight' seems to have a rather different meaning when we meet it at the close of *The Dry Salvages*, united with the images of *East Coker*: the 'wild thyme unseen' and 'winter lightning', and deprived of 'suddenness'.

> For most of us, there is only the unattended
> Moment, the moment in and out of time,
> The distraction fit, lost in a shaft of sunlight,

> The wild thyme unseen, or the winter lightning
> Or the waterfall, or music heard so deeply
> That it is not heard at all, but you are the music
> While the music lasts. These are only hints and guesses,
> Hints followed by guesses; and the rest
> Is prayer, observance, discipline, thought and action.

Here the poet seems to suggest by his tone, and by the natural images which he associates with his 'shaft of sunlight', and by the phrase 'distraction fit', and by the whole slow, rather dreamy rhythm, that these moments must not be relied on or indeed hoped for very much, but received in thankfulness as gifts when they occur. *The Dry Salvages* is a poem about ordinary people; its annunciations are the common annunciations of danger, calamity and death. It is not about special people with special gifts; it mentions the saint, only to turn back to 'most of us' who are given no special revelation, but the one Annunciation which is for all men. The image occurs here lightly and beautifully; no weight of meaning is put on to it.[1]

At the opening of *Little Gidding* this image of sunlight is totally transformed; it is made highly particular, linked with a particular season, and worked out with great descriptive detail. It is also made impersonal. The flash of winter sunlight which creates 'midwinter spring' is not a hint or a guess, or a hint followed by guesses, nor is it an almost indefinable moment of happiness, so brief that it seems perhaps an illusion; it is a revelation, apocalyptic in its intensity and brilliance:

> The brief sun flames the ice, on ponds and ditches,
> In windless cold that is the heart's heat,

[1] When Walter Hilton, at the end of the fourteenth century, a time of much mystical enthusiasm, wrote his tract *Of Angels' Song*, he did not deny that some men might truly hear wonderful sounds, though he plainly thought that a good many more thought they did and were deceived; but he concluded with some words which have the same humility as this closing section of *The Dry Salvages*: 'it sufficeth me for to live in truth principally and not in feeling.'

Reflecting in a watery mirror
A glare that is blindness in the early afternoon.
And glow more intense than blaze of branch, or brazier,
Stirs the dumb spirit: no wind, but pentecostal fire
In the dark time of the year.

The sunlight of the earlier poems has become 'frost and fire' and turns to 'flâme of incandescent terror'.

The more one reads *Four Quartets* the more these recurring images fix themselves in the mind, and through them and the changes in them we can apprehend the changing, developing subject. The yew-tree, for instance, used many times in the last three poems of *Ash Wednesday*, occurs only three times in *Four Quartets*, but each time with great and different significance. In the second verse of the lyric in *Burnt Norton*, the 'chill fingers of yew'—the touch of death hardly brushing the cheek—give us a vague sense of foreboding; at the close of *The Dry Salvages*, on the other hand, the phrase 'not too far from the yew-tree' gives a sense of security. This is the familiar yew of the churchyard, symbol both of mortality and immortality, beneath whose shade we may rest in peace. While at the end of *Little Gidding*, 'the moment of the rose and the moment of the yew-tree', the apprehension of love and the apprehension of death, are linked together, so that each seems of equal validity, an apprehension of life.

In the same way as images and symbols recur, certain words are used again and again, their meaning deepened or expanded by each fresh use. Indeed, another way of describing *Four Quartets* would be to say that the poem is an exploration of the meaning of certain words. Like the images and symbols just referred to, they are common words, words we take for granted. Perhaps the words that first strike us in this way as recurring with a special and changing emphasis are the pair 'end' and 'beginning', sometimes occurring together, sometimes apart from each other. The

word 'end' occurs first, by itself, in the opening lines of
Burnt Norton:

> What might have been and what has been
> Point to one end, which is always present.

Here 'end' has plainly some meaning beyond that of 'termi-
nation', but we are not quite certain how much meaning
to give it. Even when these two lines are repeated at the
end of the first movement, the word 'end' remains vague.
It is only in the fifth movement—when the word is linked
with 'beginning', in the context of ideas about form and
pattern and we have apparently paradoxical statements—
that we begin to think of end as meaning 'completion',
'purpose' or even 'final cause':

> Or say that the end precedes the beginning,
> And the end and the beginning were always there
> Before the beginning and after the end.
> And all is always now.

In *East Coker*, the opening inversion of Mary Stuart's
motto throws the stress on the word 'beginning' and the
whole poem ends with the word. If in *Burnt Norton* it is
'end' we are thinking of, and the word 'beginning' seems
used mainly to give meaning to 'end', in *East Coker* the
opposite is true. It is a poem about 'beginning'. On the
other hand in *The Dry Salvages* the word 'beginning' does
not occur at all, and the word 'end' is only used to be
negated. At the close of the first movement we hear of
women lying awake

> Between midnight and dawn, when the past is all deception,
> The future futureless, before the morning watch
> When time stops and time is never ending.

To stop is not to 'end'; there is no more meaning in time
stopping than in time going on. For there to be an 'end'
there must be a 'beginning', and there is no beginning

without an end. In the *sestina* the word 'end' is repeated
again and again, but only in questions and negative replies:
'Where is there an end of it?' and 'There is no end'; until
the last line points us to where both Beginning and End are
to be sought. *Little Gidding* not merely uses the words again
and again, but is full of synonyms for both, picking up one
or other of the various meanings, and it constantly translates the words into images. The refusal to speak of 'beginning' and the consequent denial of 'end' in *The Dry Salvages*
make the restoration of both words to us in the last poem
particularly moving. The tentative paradoxes of *Burnt
Norton* return with confident certainty:

> What we call the beginning is often the end
> And to make an end is to make a beginning.
> The end is where we start from.

Read in this way, with a mind alert to recognize recur-
rences—not only of words like 'end' and 'beginning', 'movement' and 'stillness', 'past', 'present' and 'future', but recur-
rences of the common prepositions and adverbs: 'before' and
'after', 'here', 'there', 'now'—the poem seems to have for
its 'thematic material' not only symbols and images, but
certain words in common use, which bring with them no
images, though they can be associated with various images.
These words receive the same kind of development as the
images do. The line from the close of *Burnt Norton*

> Quick now, here, now, always—

is as meaningless and unpoetic by itself, on a page, without
any context as Shakespeare's

> Never, never, never, never, never.

When it is repeated, right at the close of *Little Gidding*, it
gives us one of the most intense poetic experiences of the
whole poem. After all the variation and turning, the dis-

cussion and development, the subject is once more, for the last time, given us. It is given in the briefest possible way, with all adornment stripped away. For a moment, it is just as simple as that, and we knew it all the time. It is the end, and we are back at the beginning; we have had this answer before, and we recognize it as the only answer.

This musical treatment of the image, the phrase and the word, to bring out latent meanings and different significances, should prevent any reader from trying to fix the symbols in *Four Quartets*. The poem must not be read as if it were allegory, in which one 'finds values for x, y and z' and then can make the whole work out. Here one must not hunt for meanings and precise correspondencies, and because an image seems to mean something definite in one context force the same meaning on it whenever it occurs. It is obvious that the sea of *East Coker* holds a different meaning from the sea of *The Dry Salvages*. It is better in reading poetry of this kind to trouble too little about the 'meaning' than to trouble too much. If there are passages whose meaning seems elusive, where we feel we 'are missing the point', we should read on, preferably aloud; for the music and the meaning arise at 'a point of intersection', in the changes and movement of the whole. We must find meaning in the reading, rather than in any key which tells us what the rose or the yew 'stands for', or in any summary of systems of thought, whether Pre-Socratic or Christian. Reading in this way we may miss detailed significances, but the whole rhythm of the poems will not be lost, and gradually the parts will become easier for us to understand. In fact to read *Four Quartets* one must have some sense of the whole before one attempts to make very much of the parts. The sources are completely unimportant. No knowledge of the original context is required to give force to the new context. In *The Waste Land* the poet showed it was necessary to pay some regard to his sources by himself directing us to them. But we do not need to remember Tennyson's 'Mariana' when we read in *East Coker* of

> a time for the wind to break the loosened pane
> And to shake the wainscot where the field-mouse trots
> And to shake the tattered arras woven with a silent motto.

If we recognize that Mr Eliot is drawing on this favourite poem, we have pleasure in the recognition; we are not helped towards understanding what a house falling into ruin and decay is going to mean within the poem. Again, in *Little Gidding*, the initial capital and the archaic form in 'Behovely' tell us that the words 'Sin is Behovely, but all shall be well, and all manner of thing shall be well' are a quotation, and we need to realize that they have the authority of a maxim. The poet is speaking in words that are not his own, because these words are more expressive than anything he could say. We do not gain any particular help in the understanding of *Little Gidding* from knowing that the sentence comes from Julian of Norwich.

When we read *Four Quartets* in this way, attentive to this 'music of meaning', which arises at 'the point of intersection', where word relates to word, phrase to phrase, and image to image, we realize that though Mr Eliot may have given to other poets a form they can use for their own purposes, and though his treatment of the image and the word may suggest to his successors methods of developing poetic themes, *Four Quartets* is unique and essentially inimitable. In it the form is the perfect expression of the subject; so much so that one can hardly in the end distinguish subject from form. The whole poem in its unity declares more eloquently than any single line or passage that truth is not the final answer to a calculation, nor the last stage of an argument, nor something told us once and for all, which we spend the rest of our life proving by examples. The subject of *Four Quartets* is the truth which is inseparable from the way and the life in which we find it.

CHAPTER III

POETIC COMMUNICATION

Although the Word is common to all, most men live as if each had a private wisdom of his own. HERACLITUS

THE difficulty or obscurity which many readers feel in *Four Quartets* is inherent in the subject, and is not the fruit of a deliberate intention on the part of the poet. He is not intentionally writing obscurely in order to mystify, or to restrict his audience to a few like-minded persons with a special training, but is treating a subject of extreme complexity, which is constantly eluding formulation in words. Mr Eliot is, in his own words, 'occupied with frontiers of consciousness beyond which words fail, though meanings still exist'. The critic of *Four Quartets* is set a problem comparable to that which confronts the musical critic in Beethoven's last quartets, which appear to be attempting to express something which even music can hardly render, and tempt whoever tries to analyse them into using language which seems remote from music. Mr Eliot has not at the back of his mind an idea or an argument which could have been expressed quite simply, and which he is purposely disguising. These poems do not begin from an intellectual position, or a truth. They begin with a place, a point in time, and the meaning or the truth is discovered in the process of writing and in the process of reading. Each poem gathers up into itself all that has been said before, and communication becomes easier as the whole poem proceeds. That Mr Eliot is moving towards meaning and not starting from it, is shown by the comparative simplicity of *Little Gidding* when placed beside *Burnt Norton*. *Burnt Norton*, when published alone, seemed almost impenetrably obscure, and is much easier to understand when one has read the remainder of the sequence; but *Little Gidding* can be understood by itself, without reference to the preceding poems, which it yet so beautifully completes. There is progress throughout *Four Quartets* towards an 'easy commerce', a freedom in communication, which does not necessarily make *Little Gidding* in its clarity a better poem than *Burnt Norton* is in its obscurity, but does give us a sense of completion, that what was to be said has now at last been said.

The progress is from abstract thinking, and an intensely personal experience—so personal and private that it becomes almost impersonal, the private incommunicable experience of all men—to the concrete, the established in place, time and circumstances, and the general, the common experience which persons can share to some extent with each other. In *Burnt Norton* the actual place is hardly described at all. Critics have spoken of the seventeenth-century manor house and its garden, but as far as we can learn from the poem it might be any house and garden in the country, into which we might wander idly and feel a passing curiosity about the people who had lived there. There is nothing to suggest that the house has any particular beauty or interest and the garden is simply a conventional formal garden, now deserted.[1] We hardly know how much of the detail is memory, imagination of what might have been, or external present fact. This is a poem about the 'private world' of each one of us, the world in which what might have been

[1] I stress this because in an article in *New Writing and Daylight* (Summer 1942), written before the publication of *Little Gidding*, I wrongly suggested, on the analogy of *East Coker* and *The Dry Salvages*, that the house in *Burnt Norton* might also be connected with Mr Eliot's family. The suggestion sprang from an incomplete appreciation of *Burnt Norton*, and I hope I should have in time realized my mistake, even if I had not been corrected by Mr Eliot in a letter.

persists in the consciousness as well as what was, and in which the life that was actually lived by unknown people in a strange house is less real than the life we might have lived there ourselves, with our own family, if things had been different.[1] This 'private world', so intensely real to each of us individually, can hardly be communicated; it lies deep beneath the personality which others know. The difficulty of communication is reflected in the uncertain use of the personal pronouns. Mainly an impersonal plural is used: 'we', 'our', 'us'; and when, only twice, 'I' is used, it is used diffidently, in quasi-negative statements:

> My words echo
> Thus, in your mind.
> But to what purpose
> Disturbing the dust on a bowl of rose-leaves
> I do not know.

And later:

> I can only say, *there* we have been: but I cannot say where.
> And I cannot say, how long, for that is to place it in time.

In *East Coker*, on the other hand, the village is described, and there is throughout a strong sense of a particular person speaking. We are told of family ties, of persons living together in a community, and at the beginning of the last movement, we feel no uncertainty in the poet's voice as he speaks to us of himself, directly: 'So here I am, in the middle way.' The 'we' of *East Coker* is used for generalization from personal experience, not in order to escape from the personal; and the 'you' addressed in the first movement—'if you do not come too close, if you do not come too close' —is singular: a person is speaking to a person, to the

---

[1] Compare Harry in *The Family Reunion*:
I was not there, you were not there, only our phantasms
And what did not happen is as true as what did happen
O my dear, and you walked through the little door
And I ran to meet you in the rose-garden.

individual listener or reader. *East Coker* is of all four poems the most personal, the most concerned with 'I', a person of a certain family, with a certain history, trying to write poetry at a certain time and under particular conditions. By contrast *The Dry Salvages* seems general. It passes quickly from the opening 'I do not know much about gods' to the plural pronouns, and though the third movement opens again with the tentative 'I sometimes wonder if that is what Krishna meant', it also quickly leaves the singular. The characteristic pronoun of *The Dry Salvages* is 'we', and the 'you' addressed in the third movement is a plural 'you'. *The Dry Salvages* is full of anonymous crowds, the fishermen, the voyagers, the anxious worried women, the passengers on trains and liners; we do not think so much of particular destinies as of the common lot, and the poet places himself among these undistinguished figures. But in *Little Gidding* the poet passes easily from singular to plural, beginning with the familiar

> If you came this way,
> Taking the route you would be likely to take,

where each of us is addressed, and varying from the personal conversation of the colloquy with the 'dead master' to the natural use of the plural in the last movement. Communication seems perfectly established in this last poem, where place and time are fully and vividly described, and the personages referred to are not merely members of the poet's family or the vast unindividualized crowds of *The Dry Salvages*, but persons of history, who have meaning for us as much as for the poet, and whose lives and actions are fruitful in our lives as well as in his. *Little Gidding* has no characteristic pronoun; the poet passes as in conversation from one to another, without diffidence, or the deliberate evasion of the personal or the general by the use of the pronoun 'one', on which he falls back in *East Coker*.

This variation in the use of the personal pronouns from *Burnt Norton* to *Little Gidding* is a sign of the difficulty of Mr Eliot's enterprise. He is writing of religious experience, of how the mind comes to discover religious truth: truth which interprets for us our whole experience of life. But he is doing this in an age which has no universally or even widely-held conscious formulation of belief; and even more important for a poet (for poetry has more in common with worship than with philosophy and theology) no accepted tradition of worship, expressing itself in a familiar ritual and liturgy. This predicament is glanced at in the Greek quotation from Heraclitus, which stands as one of the epigraphs to *Four Quartets*, and which I have put at the head of this chapter: 'Although the Word is common to all, most men live as if each had a private wisdom of his own.' If the poet speaks from his private wisdom, how can his readers each with their own private wisdoms find in him 'the Word which is common to all'? The religious poet today cannot rely upon a common fund of religious imagery and religious symbolism, upon liturgical phrases, and great sayings from the Scriptures, to which each of his readers can bring his own private wisdom and experience. These have become, if not a private wisdom, at least a kind of *coterie* wisdom in the circumstances of today. Where Langland in *Piers Plowman* calls upon the common religious emotions of his readers by his use of Latin sentences from the Breviary and Missal, which provide continual points of reference for his reader, by which he may follow and share in the poet's bold speculations and intensely personal visions, the modern poet is likely to estrange many of his readers if he employs words and symbols which are connected with beliefs they do not share. A phrase which is full of meaning to him, and to those accustomed to use it or hear it in the same context, may to others seem a mere piece of pious jargon. The lack of con-

tact between the traditional language of Christian worship
and prayer and the most vigorous and lively writing in
prose and poetry today makes a liturgical phrase seem in-
trusive. An age which has hardly produced a hymn which
can be sung without embarrassment, and displays in its
attempts to supplement the Litany and to provide special
collects and services for national occasions its inability to
assimilate traditional diction and rhythms with modern, is
not an age in which a poet can use without self-consciousness the language of the Bible and Prayer Book. In *Ash
Wednesday* Mr Eliot, in Langland's fashion, employed
phrases from the prayers and liturgies of the Church. But it
is very doubtful whether these phrases fulfilled their proper
poetic function, except for a small minority of readers. I
think they were felt as an irritant by the majority, to whom
they brought no real associations of prayer and worship, but
merely the suggestion of conventional religious phrase-
ology.[1] The method in *Four Quartets* is completely different,
and just as the sensitive variation in the use of pronouns
shows us the poet feeling his way towards intimacy with
his audience, so his use of specifically religious words and
symbols shows a scrupulous care. Outside the lyric fourth
movement, he employs them only at certain climaxes, where
they occur with remarkable effect.

[1] The most remarkable demonstration I have had of this failure in communication in *Ash Wednesday* was at a tea-party, when a colleague said that
the repetition at the close of Section III always suggested to him a drunk man
coming home late at night and muttering to himself as he stumbled up the
stairs. When someone present objected: 'But it is a phrase from the Canon of
the Mass', he replied: 'How am I supposed to know that; it doesn't mean
anything to me.' When someone else added: 'But surely you recognize it as
coming from the New Testament?', he answered: 'Well, lots of phrases come
out of the Bible ultimately.' Even for those who accept the Christian Faith
some of the phrases in *Ash Wednesday* have less than their full effect, for to
feel their force one needs to be accustomed to use them in the same context
as the poet. I have sometimes felt that only those presented on the occasion
of their Confirmation with that popular manual of devotion, *St Swithun's
Prayer Book*, read *Ash Wednesday* with a natural response to the poet's intention.

In *Burnt Norton* the poet has deliberately discarded any help he might obtain from the formulations of the Church, in his attempt to call upon the 'private wisdom' of each of us. The experience of *Burnt Norton* can be given a religious interpretation, and could have been described in religious terms, but the poet does not provide any explanation, nor does he employ any religious phrases, until, nearly at the close, in what is a kind of parenthesis, he speaks of 'the Word in the desert', and takes us to the first chapter of the Gospel of St John, and to the Synoptic narratives of the Temptation in the Wilderness. But the effect is quite different from the effect in *Ash Wednesday*, where the private meditation is transformed into the ageless prayer of the Church. Here it is more as if two worlds suddenly for a moment touch, and we see that what the poet has been speaking of is what Christians speak of in another language. He has been speaking of words, and suddenly we are reminded that the Evangelist adopted from Greek philosophy the conception of the Word or Logos, as the origin and root of all things, and that Christians believe that this Word became flesh and was subject to the tension of life in time, which words suffer. In *East Coker*, twice and without preparation, the single, awful and undefined word 'God' is used; in the second movement where the poet breaks out with

> Do not let me hear
> Of the wisdom of old men, but rather of their folly,
> Their fear of fear and frenzy, their fear of possession,
> Of belonging to another, or to others, or to God;

and again in the third:

> I said to my soul, be still, and let the dark come upon you
> Which shall be the darkness of God.

We feel here that the poet could use no other word. He is speaking of our experience of the 'Other', what is not ourselves. He cannot here avoid this great word, by which men have expressed their sense that behind otherness there is One who is Other. It is not until *The Dry Salvages* that words of precise Christian significance are used, and the first of these, the word 'annunciation', in the second movement, is put back at first from its special Christian meaning into common speech:

> The prayer of the bone on the beach, the unprayable
> Prayer at the calamitous annunciation;

and again:

> The silent listening to the undeniable
> Clamour of the bell of the last annunciation.

Only in the last verse of the *sestina* is it restored to a religious use, with the capital that takes us to Galilee and the Virgin's house at Nazareth and the

> hardly, barely prayable
> Prayer of the one Annunciation.

On the other hand, without preparation, but with extraordinary force, the single theological word in all four poems occurs in the fifth movement:

> These are only hints and guesses,
> Hints followed by guesses; and the rest
> Is prayer, observance, discipline, thought and action.
> The hint half guessed, the gift half understood, is Incarnation.

Coming as it does, this word is in itself a true 'point of intersection'; for the Christian reader, who is accustomed to meditate upon the mystery, a familiar doctrine is made strange, while for the non-Christian reader, who has followed the poet with sympathy so far, a new possibility of meaning is suggested in a language and way of thought he had regarded as obsolete. After this the poet can quite naturally employ the language of the Christian life in *Little*

Gidding, and speak of 'prayer' and 'a secluded chapel' and 'sin' with simplicity.[1]

In the fourth lyric movement, as we should expect, the emotion of each poem crystallizes itself and demands expression in concrete terms; but even here the poet does not allow himself to use the language of Christian worship until *The Dry Salvages.* In *Burnt Norton,* the lyric is totally untheological, and describes simply an experience of what appears to be indefinable except as a kind of stillness in which there is expectancy. In *East Coker,* on the other hand, the lyric expounds to us the mystery of the Cross. But it does so without using any of the terms or metaphors by which the great Doctors, beginning with St Paul, have attempted to make that mystery apprehensible. The great words, atonement, redemption, salvation, are not employed; nor are we given the religious metaphor of the High Priest making sacrifice, or the legal metaphors of a ransom paid or a debt cancelled. Instead we have the metaphor of a hospital. This poem has been elucidated in some detail by Mr Preston.[2] I do not wish to quarrel with his interpretation, but I think its method a little obscures what Mr Eliot has done in this profoundly moving poem. I am not happy at the suggestion that 'the *dying nurse* is presumably the Church militant' or that 'the *ruined millionaire* is Adam', even though Mr Preston gives Mr Eliot as his authority for this last identification. The poem is not an allegory, and precise annotation of this kind may destroy the imaginative power of this restatement of the cost of salvation. The only explicitly theological phrase is 'Adam's curse', and

---

[1] 'Prayer' in *Little Gidding,* as in the last stanza of the *sestina* and in the fifth movement of *The Dry Salvages,* means prayer as a religious exercise. At the beginning of the *sestina* it is used metaphorically. The change in the use of the word in the last stanza is a parallel to the change in the use of the word 'Annunciation'.

[2] See Raymond Preston *Four Quartets Rehearsed* (1947).

that is after all a phrase in common use. We all know that Adam, that is all mankind, must labour for his bread in sorrow and must die. The words 'purgatorial fires' need not be interpreted precisely, and the wonderful line:

Of which the flame is roses, and the smoke is briars,

is made less vivid by an attempt to fix the symbolism of the rose in Christian art. It speaks of an extremity of pain in which there are moments of ecstasy, when through the stifling smoke there drifts for a moment the poignant wild smell of briars. The 'wounded surgeon', the 'dying nurse', the 'ruined millionaire' are to me all the same figure under different terms. I would rather suggest to those who asked me to explain this poem that they should read the fifty-third chapter of *Isaiah* or the second chapter of *Philippians*, and think over the prophet's conception of the 'suffering servant', or the doctrine of the Son of God 'emptying himself', than that they should try to work out distinctions between these types of self-forgetful compassion, of suffering united with the power to help and comfort sufferers, of generosity without limit.[1] We need not introduce the difficult conception of Original Sin; we do better to think about the meaning of the word 'hospital'. A hospital is both a place to die in and a place to be cured in, and perhaps to be cured is to die; every recovery is a kind of death, and to die is our only final cure. To endow a hospital may be a great act of charity, and to suffer in it or to help the suffering may equally be acts of love. Patient and surgeon, nurse and dying man, millionaire and the poorest beggar admitted in the casual ward, are not separated in this hospital the poet speaks of—one giving, the other receiving. In this place of pain it is a wounded surgeon who

[1] Mr Preston seems to think that to be a millionaire is in itself evil. Perhaps it is, but we are not to think here in terms of the capitalist system, but only in terms of boundless wealth.

resolves the enigma of what is otherwise a mere record of delirious terrors, a dying nurse whose authority is recognized and obeyed by the dying, and a ruined millionaire whose charity is not an offence to the suffering. The phrase at the end of the lyric: 'In spite of that, we call this Friday good', gives us the same kind of shock as the use of the word 'Annunciation' in *The Dry Salvages*. For the whole lyric has shown us how awful and paradoxical is this common Bank Holiday name. Without thinking we call the day on which the Son of Man suffered and died, not 'Black Friday', but 'Good Friday'. The lyric in *East Coker* expounds *East Coker*'s own phrase; it is a poem on the darkness 'which shall be the darkness of God'. In *The Dry Salvages*, where we find the Christian terms Annunciation and Incarnation employed, the lyric uses boldly the language of Christian prayer. It is a prayer to Our Lady, addressed in Dante's words as 'Figlia del tuo figlio', and as Queen of Heaven. It is impersonal, the prayer of ordinary men engaged in ordinary business, who live by faith, and whose lives are given value not by any rare or remarkable experience of their own, but by their belief. It is the prayer of those who hardly pray themselves. The hymn in *Little Gidding* is again different. Although it begins with the Pentecostal image of the descending dove in tongues of flame, and although it continues in language whose slight formality and tinge of Latinity recalls the style of eighteenth-century hymns, it is nearer to the lyric of *East Coker* than to the prayer of *The Dry Salvages*. It declares the truth of the Christian experience that God is Love, and expounds the mysterious 'All shall be well' and the closing phrase of the whole poem: 'the fire and the rose are one'.

In an essay on Pascal, Mr Eliot says of Montaigne that 'he succeeded in giving expression to the scepticism of *every* human being' and adds: 'For every man who thinks and lives by thought must have his own scepticism, that which stops at the question, that which ends in denial, or that which leads to faith and which is somehow integrated into the faith which transcends it.' If *Four Quartets* shows scepticism integrated into faith, it shows scepticism none the less; and in a sceptical age it speaks to those whose scepticism stops at the question, and to those who are led to denial, as well as those who are led to believe. It is not the poet's business to make us believe *what* he believes, but to make us believe *that* he believes. He must convince us that he is himself convinced. He must also convince us that what he believes genuinely interprets, makes sense of, experience which we recognize as our own. Although we may not accept his interpretation, we must feel it is a real interpretation. In an age like ours, with no accepted system of belief, in which the traditional system is not so much actively disbelieved as ignored, such an interpretation can only convince if the poet forgoes what earlier Christian writers have loved to employ: the language of the Bible and of the common prayers of the Church.

The problem of communication for a religious poet in an age where his religious beliefs are not widely held is a special aspect of the general problem of communication for the poet in the modern world. Until about a hundred years ago the public for whom a poet wrote was, if not so compact and unified culturally as is sometimes suggested, at least in rough agreement as to what an educated man should be presumed to know. Obviously not all the courtiers who listened to Chaucer reading his poems, nor all the readers for whom Caxton printed *The Canterbury Tales* can have been aware of the width of Chaucer's reading, or recognized the varied sources he was drawing on; but the kind of learning Chaucer had—in the classics, in old and new medieval poetry, in the discipline of rhetoric—was the kind of learning expected of a poet; a kind of learning to which educated men aspired. In the same way not all Milton's readers can have recognized all his classical allusions, or been able to complete at once the story of a myth he referred to in passing, but in general his readers regarded Greek and Latin poetry as the proper study in schools and universities. If, among familiar allusions, there were some that were remote, the audience did not feel irritated by the poet's superiority in culture. The less well-educated reader, aware that he was less well-educated, did not blame the poet for displaying a deeper knowledge, nor resent his possessing it. The modern poet is in a very different position. The reading public is far larger, the output of printed matter incomparably greater, and the content of education has expanded so enormously that there is now no general cultural tradition to which the poet can refer or be referred. The divisions do not only run between those who are trained in the scientific disciplines and those trained in the humanities; but between science and science and between one branch of the humanities and another. The development of English Literature and Modern Languages as academic subjects has had something to do with making communication more difficult for the modern poet than for his ancestor, for whom the humanities meant Greek and Latin. Many poets have been inspired to a greater or less degree by their reading. The inspiration is not usually sought deliberately; it happens by accidents of education and environment and even more by some need in the individual temperament of the poet. Something read stays in the memory, provokes a train of thought, stimulates a rhythm. Sometimes this influence is so compelling that the poet has to imitate and finds to some extent his own voice through another's. But when an author is deeply read in minor Jacobean drama and a reader is equally at home in Corneille and Racine, but has little knowledge of English drama beyond a school study of a few plays of Shakespeare, full communication is less likely than when both are well versed in Virgil, Horace and Shakespeare. The Jacobean tone will irritate rather than please. It will seem a deliberate, even pretentious, imitation; whereas the Virgilian reference of the older poets gave delight, because it put the reader and the poet into a sympathetic relation through a common admiration. Pope began his career on better terms with his audience than any equally literary poet can hope to be today.

The lack of a common shared background of reading and literary tradition affects some poets more than others. But poets are born before they are made, and must write according to their temperaments and tastes. Part of the difficulty of Mr Eliot's early work arose from what he has described himself as 'an intense and narrow taste determined by personal needs'. This early taste led him to the later Elizabethan dramatists for a style of great rhetorical force, and to the French symbolists for a manner that allowed him to express an intensely individual view of life with the minimum of direct statement. The personal need was in his temperament—ironic, diffident, at war with his surroundings; sceptical, preferring understatement, hints and suggestions; fastidious, reserved, acutely sensitive to beauty and ugliness, but even more to misery and happiness. This temperament made the symbolists congenial, for their method of finding an 'objective correlative' for emotional states gave him an opportunity to write with a clarity, precision and expressiveness which satisfied his poetic taste, while it allowed him to escape from the lyric poet's necessity of speaking either for himself or for all men. J. Alfred Prufrock's love song is neither personal, nor general, though in it the poet expresses a personal vision, and defines what is perhaps a general predicament. The originality, however, lies in the blend of this oblique manner with a highly passionate and dramatic style, which constantly escapes from the regions of wit, irony and sensibility into a dramatic intensity of feeling. This tension between treatment and style, which gives the early poetry much of its disturbing power and beauty, was one of the things which made it difficult for the ordinary reader to see what the poet was 'getting at'. The difficulty, however, lay not only in an unfamiliar manner and an unfamilar style, and their mixture to produce the original combination of an apparently strictly limited subject and an unlimited linguistic daring. A more serious difficulty was the poet's assumption that his readers could supply from their own experience, and particularly from their reading, what he chose to leave unsaid, or only hint at. The private invented symbols present in most cases no difficulty. We know what Sweeney, Prufrock, Burbank with his Baedeker and Bleistein with his fat cigar, and the haggard Princess Volupine stand for,[1] though Pipit with her knitting has been very variously interpreted. (She has been convincingly identified to me at different times, as the poet's aged nurse, his lower-middle-class mistress, and a nice young lady he once thought of proposing to.) But even with the help of the jumble of quotations in the epigraph, how many readers without a literary education are aware unassisted of the Shakespearian references that underlie and give point to the briefly sketched story of Princess Volupine and her favours; and what person without rather specialized theological interests could explain why it is Origen who comes to Mr Eliot's mind at his Sunday Morning Service as he watches the bees through the window-pane, and could annotate the phrase 'at the mensual turn of time'? This habit of literary allusion

---

[1] The genius for inventing names shown in the early volumes finds scope in the later verse only in *Old Possum's Book of Practical Cats*.

is far more marked in *The Waste Land*, where Mr Eliot, anticipating the professors, supplied some of his own notes. But the reader needs far more than a note in many places. When we have straight parody, as in the re-writing of 'When lovely woman stoops to folly' or in

> The sound of horns and motors, which shall bring
> Sweeney to Mrs Porter in the spring,

a note can help us as it does when we are reading *The Dunciad*; but a mere reference to a scene and act in *The Spanish Tragedy* will not take us very far towards the understanding of what Hieronymo's 'Why then Ile fit you' means at the close of *The Waste Land*, and we really need to know *The White Devil* familiarly as well as *The Golden Bough* to receive the proper poetic shock at the twisted quotation in

> That corpse you planted last year in your garden,
> Has it begun to sprout? Will it bloom this year?
> Or has the sudden frost disturbed its bed?
> Oh keep the Dog far hence, that's friend to men,
> Or with his nails he'll dig it up again!

We have, I need hardly say, no right to complain of a poet's being difficult, and to insist that he must be comprehensible to the average reader without any special trouble. Nor is being difficult a merit in itself. We have to read poetry on the poet's own terms, and the poet is perfectly at liberty to write if he chooses for 'fit audience though few', just as the reader is perfectly at liberty not to read him. There have always been difficult poets, though they have not always been met with the same hostility as is shown to them today, when the difficult poet is blamed for superiority rather than admired for ingenuity. But the difficulty of *Four Quartets* is different from the difficulty of the earlier poetry. Although there is a good deal of literary reminiscence in it, and although the reader who recognizes it gains an added pleasure, we are not hindered from understanding the poem by failure to recall the original context of words or lines. Ultimately the difficulty in both the early and the later poetry arises from the nature of the poet's subject, which he can only express, he feels, in this way. But a certain change in the subject-matter has led to a change in the style and treatment, and the most obvious way of describing the change is to say that in *Four Quartets* one is aware of a perpetual effort towards communication, a desire to speak plainly, where before one was aware of the poet's desire to avoid direct statement, by the use of various 'Masks', and by the habit of allusion. Where the early style is concise, condensed, and tends towards the cryptic and oracular, the later is diffuse, repetitive, and tends towards the familiar.

This change of style is obviously connected with Mr Eliot's attempts to write verse drama. He has been to school to an audience instead of a reading public. However intense and deep dramatic poetry may be, it must have a certain clarity of surface meaning. Although it may make allusions that few of the audience notice, it must not rely on them. But the attempts to write verse drama are in themselves a sign of a change in Mr Eliot's attitude towards his subject and his public. The concluding chapter of *The Use of Poetry* is interesting here:

The difficulty of poetry may be due to one of several reasons. First, there may be personal causes which make it impossible for a poet to express himself in any but an obscure way; while this may be regrettable, we should be glad, I think, that the man has been able to express himself at all. Or difficulty may be due just to novelty. . . . Or difficulty may be caused by the reader's having been told, or having suggested to himself, that the poem is going to prove difficult . . . And finally, there is the difficulty caused by the author's having left something out which the reader is used to finding; so that the reader, bewildered, gropes about for what is absent, and puzzles his head for a kind of 'meaning' which is not there, and is not meant to be there.

While both the earlier and the later poetry have the difficulty of novelty, the main reason for the difficulty of the early poetry is, I think, the first one given: that the poet can only express himself obscurely; and the main reason why the later poetry is felt to be difficult is the last: that people try to read it in the wrong way. The early poetry needs elucidation and annotation; the later poetry needs simply to be read again and again until we become familiar with its manner. Mr Eliot went on to say:

> When all exceptions have been made, and after admitting the possible existence of minor 'difficult' poets whose public must always be small, I believe that the poet naturally prefers to write for as large and miscellaneous an audience as possible, and that it is the half-educated and ill-educated, rather than the uneducated, who stand in his way: I myself should like an audience which could neither read nor write. The most useful poetry, socially, would be one which could cut across all the present stratifications of public taste—stratifications which are perhaps a sign of social disintegration. The ideal medium for poetry, to my mind, and the most direct means of social 'usefulness' for poetry, is the theatre.

Although we may feel that Mr Eliot has in mind the Platonic Idea of an illiterate audience, rather than any illiterate audience a poet is likely to encounter today, the confession of a desire to write for a large and miscellaneous audience is a striking one from the poet of *The Waste Land*; and the hope that poetry may overleap the stratifications of public taste reveals also a change of purpose. This lecture was delivered in the winter of 1932–3, and it suggests that Mr Eliot's writing of *The Rock* (performed in 1934 in aid of the Forty-five Churches Fund of the Diocese of London) and of *Murder in the Cathedral* (written for the Festival of the Friends of Canterbury Cathedral in 1935) had behind it not simply the desire to employ his talents in the service of the Church, but this other desire to write for a miscellaneous audience. The audience who went to Sadler's Wells to see

The Rock, or to the Canterbury Festival for *Murder in the Cathedral*, was largely, one supposes, composed of church-goers, who, though united in belief, represent a wide cross-section of the public culturally. Those who read *The Waste Land*, on the other hand, may have had every divergence of belief, but they were united in possessing literary culture. The two commissioned works were, in fact, necessary steps towards *The Family Reunion* and *Four Quartets*; for in them, while the poet limited his audience in one way, he enlarged it in another, and developed a new tone of voice.

Just as in *Four Quartets* Mr Eliot has, for the sake of his miscellaneous audience, shown a scrupulous sensitiveness in the use of religious terms, so in his choice of simple and common symbols, in his repetitions and fresh starts, we are aware of him speaking as a man to men, without particular distinctions. The effort towards full expression—the 'intolerable wrestle with words and meanings'—leads him to passages that are in themselves flat, prosaic and inexpressive, when he turns round upon himself, sometimes with a kind of wry humour as in *East Coker*, where he comments:

> That was a way of putting it—not very satisfactory:
> A periphrastic study in a worn-out poetical fashion,
> Leaving one still with the intolerable wrestle
> With words and meanings. The poetry does not matter.
> It was not (to start again) what one had expected. . . .

Or again he can be tentative, as in *The Dry Salvages*, where he hazards the suggestion:

> I sometimes wonder if that is what Krishna meant—
> Among other things—or one way of putting the same thing:

or at times he can be slightly incoherent, involving himself in parenthesis and lack of grammatical sequence, with a consciousness in his tone that he is rather talking round his subject and letting his mind circle:

It seems, as one becomes older,
That the past has another pattern, and ceases to be a mere
    sequence—
Or even development: the latter a partial fallacy
Encouraged by superficial notions of evolution,
Which becomes, in the popular mind, a means of disowning
    the past.
The moments of happiness—not the sense of well-being,
Fruition, fulfilment, security or affection,
Or even a very good dinner, but the sudden illumination—
We had the experience but missed the meaning,
And approach to the meaning restores the experience
In a different form, beyond any meaning
We can assign to happiness.

These passages play their part in the musical economy of the poem; they represent a change of voice, the mind relaxing, a new approach to a theme already handled in another way, or a hint or a guess at a theme that is coming. But they also contribute very largely to that final impression of integrity and sincerity which is the reward of the poet's effort towards communication.

Nothing could show better the change in Mr Eliot's manner than to place side by side the conclusion of *The Waste Land* and the conclusion of *Four Quartets*. Each is the fitting climax to all that has gone before, and each has its own peculiar beauty as a conclusion. There will probably always be readers who prefer one manner to the other; just as with lovers of Milton there are those who prefer *Paradise Lost* to *Samson Agonistes*, and others who, for all their admiration for *Paradise Lost*, find *Samson Agonistes* the more satisfying and profounder work. At the close of *The Waste Land* the poet speaks as the fisherman, with the arid plains behind him, and he illuminates his predicament by his reference to the prayer of Jacopone da Todi, sometimes set before the *Purgatorio*: 'Set my love in order, O thou who lovest me.' The most he can conceive of doing is the setting of his *lands* in order, for the ordering of his love is beyond his power. And then, as the poet runs off into quotation, the figure of the fisherman fades, and the poet's own voice is lost. We end with many voices in different languages and from different centuries, with enigmatic commands, and a final benediction in an ancient unknown tongue. The reader of *The Waste Land* must possess, to appreciate it, a historic sense, and a literary culture, which can make such references alive to him. He must be the kind of person to whom quotation is a natural means of expression. But at the close of *Little Gidding* there is no need of any special knowledge. We hear the poet's own voice, the voice of a person who does not find it easy to speak out, but who speaks to us here with simplicity.

CHAPTER IV

THE DRY SEASON

> I will show you fear in a handful of dust.
> *The Waste Land*

Canst thou lift up thy voice to the clouds, that abundance of waters may cover thee? Canst thou send lightnings that they may go, and say unto thee, Here we are? *Job*, XXXVIII, 34-5

THE contrast, striking and obvious as it is, between the matter and manner of *The Waste Land* and of *Four Quartets* is, like every true contrast, made possible by an underlying sameness. When *Ash Wednesday* first appeared the contrast with the earlier poetry naturally impressed readers most. It seemed as if Mr Eliot had broken with his own past. But the development of the new style, coming to perfection in *Four Quartets*, makes it possible to see what unites his earlier and his later poetry, and makes all his work unmistakably the product of the same personality, expressing itself in a voice, which, though its tones alter, is still the same voice. The essential unity of his poetry, in spite of change and development, arises from the integrity with which he has explored his own vision of life. His poetic career has shown to a high degree the quality that Keats called 'negative capability', when a man is 'capable of being in uncertainties, mysteries, doubts, without any irritable reaching after fact and reason'. He has never forced his poetic voice, but has been content with 'hints and guesses'. His development has been a growth in the understanding of his earlier experience, not a rejection of it. The source of his poetry does not change, though his attitude towards it alters. From the beginning he is a poet who feels profoundly 'the inadequacy of our state to our conceptions'.[1]

---

[1] The phrase is Byron's, speaking of the hero of his *Cain*.

In the chapter on Matthew Arnold in *The Use of Poetry* there are two remarks, both outbursts of irritation at Arnold, which are very revealing. Mr Eliot seems to have been provoked into abandoning his usual reticence about the subject of his poetry. In the first he is commenting upon Arnold's statement in his discussion of Burns that 'no one can deny that it is of advantage to a poet to deal with a beautiful world', and he observes:

It is an advantage to mankind in general to live in a beautiful world; that no one can doubt. But for the poet is it so important? We mean all sorts of things, I know, by Beauty. But the essential advantage for a poet is not, to have a beautiful world with which to deal: it is to be able to see beneath both beauty and ugliness; to see the boredom, and the horror, and the glory. The vision of the horror and the glory was denied to Arnold, but he knew something of the boredom.

The second remark is a retort to Arnold's famous *dictum* that 'Poetry is at bottom a criticism of life', on which Mr Eliot comments:

At bottom: that is a great way down; the bottom is the bottom. At the bottom of the abyss is what few ever see, and what those cannot bear to look at for long; and it is not 'a criticism of life'. If we mean life as a whole—not that Arnold ever saw life as a whole —from top to bottom, can anything that we can say of it ultimately, of that awful mystery, be called criticism? We bring back very little from our rare descents, and that is not criticism.

I do not wish to discuss whether this is wholly fair to Arnold. It may also be objected that there are some great poets—Chaucer for instance—who cannot be thought of in this way. The importance of the passage lies in the phrase 'the boredom, and the horror, and the glory', which seems a summary of the development of Mr Eliot's vision of the world. It is the middle term which is of most interest and which helps us to understand the essential unity of his work. Up to *The Waste Land* the movement is from what might be called boredom to something that might be called terror, alternating with its more disinterested companion, horror; or, more truly, since terror and horror are present from the beginning, the poetry shows a deepening sense of horror in which boredom is swallowed up. The later poetry shows a movement from terror or horror towards glimpses of glory. Again, more truly, there is not so much a movement as a fuller discovery in horror of a glory by which horror gradually fades. To use another term, what unites the earlier and the later poetry is the consciousness of 'the abyss'.

In *Prufrock and Other Observations*, and in *Poems* (1920) we are mainly conscious of the boredom:

> One thinks of all the hands
> That are raising dingy shades
> In a thousand furnished rooms.

The *taedium vitae* could hardly be expressed more concisely than in lines like these, or in images of staleness such as:

> sunless dry geraniums
> And dust in crevices,
> Smells of chestnuts in the streets,
> And female smells in shuttered rooms,
> And cigarettes in corridors
> And cocktail smells in bars.

In these early poems, as throughout Mr Eliot's poetry, images of taste and smell are remarkably frequent. Taste and smell are the most immediate of our senses, and the least translatable into intellectual terms by the conscious mind. They are also the most at the mercy of the external world, for we can avert our eyes, stop our ears, and refrain from touching more easily than we can escape a smell, which is haunting and pervasive.[1] Such images are natural

---

[1] Compare Harry in *The Family Reunion*:

> Do you feel a kind of stirring underneath the air?
> Do you? don't you? a communication, a scent
> Direct to the brain . . .

to a poet whose subject is something 'beneath both beauty and ugliness'.

The sense of the infinite weariness of life, its stale sameness, is combined with a rather 'literary' horror in certain images, which recall self-consciously decadent poetry. I have never been very frightened by

> Midnight shakes the memory
> As a madman shakes a dead geranium;

though the picture of the daft moon is disquieting:

> She winks a feeble eye,
> She smiles into corners.
> She smooths the hair of the grass.
> The moon has lost her memory.
> A washed-out smallpox cracks her face,
> Her hand twists a paper rose,
> That smells of dust and eau de Cologne,
> She is alone
> With all the old nocturnal smells
> That cross and cross across her brain.

The genuine horror is in images which are not fantastic or romantically terrifying, but display the horror which inhabits the stale, the monotonous, the wearisomely repetitive:

> The worlds revolve like ancient women
> Gathering fuel in vacant lots.

The automatic, meaningless act suddenly appears an act of terror; it turns into a desperate act:

> 'Remark the cat which flattens itself in the gutter,
> Slips out its tongue
> And devours a morsel of rancid butter.'
> So the hand of the child, automatic,
> Slipped out and pocketed a toy that was running along the quay.
> I could see nothing behind that child's eye.
> I have seen eyes in the street
> Trying to peer through lighted shutters,
> And a crab one afternoon in a pool,
> An old crab with barnacles on his back,
> Gripped the end of a stick which I held him.

Or the sense of meaninglessness can be blended with acute self-disgust and sheer panic in such a haunting image as

> I should have been a pair of ragged claws
> Scuttling across the floors of silent seas.

The epigraph to Prufrock's love-song might have stood as an epigraph to the whole volume. When Guido de Montefeltro in the penultimate circle of 'that blind world' consents to speak with Dante, a hopeless soul is speaking to another whom he believes to be hopeless also:

> For that is ones in helle out cometh it neuere;
> Job the prophete, patriarke, reproueth thi sawes,
> *Quia in inferno nulla est redempcio.*

This sense of the boredom and the horror behind both beauty and ugliness is expressed also by the trick, learned partly from Ezra Pound, of juxtaposing the beautiful and the ugly, the heroic and the sordid, and makes it more than a trick. Sometimes only a simple contrast seems intended. In 'Sweeney Erect' the splendid Jacobean opening, which gives us a wild and beautiful setting for the mythical figures of the forsaken Ariadne and the perjured fleeing Theseus, is an ironic prelude to the verses describing what happens in Mrs Turner's 'hotel'—where Sweeney gets up to shave, his lady-friend has hysterics on the bed, and, in place of the God Bacchus descending to comfort a forsaken princess, Doris pads in from her bath, with a glass of sal-volatile and a stiff brandy. But in 'Sweeney among the Nightingales' the last verses give 'a last twist of the knife' beyond the simple contrast of the heroic past and the trivial present:

> The host with someone indistinct
> Converses at the door apart,
> The nightingales are singing near
> The Convent of the Sacred Heart,

And sang within the bloody wood
When Agamemnon cried aloud,
And let their liquid siftings fall
To stain the stiff dishonoured shroud.

The exquisite song which pours from the nightingales'
throats and the 'liquid siftings', which they let fall with the
same indifference and unconcern, accompany alike the death
of Agamemnon, King of Kings, and this sordid plot against
Sweeney. It is equally significant or insignificant whether it
is Agamemnon who is betrayed and murdered or Sweeney,
and there is no more relevance in the nightingales' lovely
song than in their casual droppings. We call one beautiful
and the other ugly; they are both irrelevant to our disasters.
It is perhaps an illusion that we should think the death of
Agamemnon important and the death of Sweeney sordid.
The nightingales make no such distinction. The stars are as
menacing over South America as over Argos; but the
portents seem absurd if this is all they portend: a conspiracy
in a low dive.

There are many other aspects of these early poems,
which have been sufficiently commented upon: their witty
ingenuity, their stylistic maturity, their complex rather
mannered sophistication, their power of phrasing that makes
them so immensely quotable. Their extraordinary versa-
tility, however, only emphasizes their common ground.
Throughout both volumes we are aware of the 'sense of the
abyss'. There is an 'overwhelming question', which is not
being asked; which one dare not ask, for perhaps there is no
answer or only such an answer as it would be better not to
know. Aunt Helen, with her harmless existence, Cousin
Nancy with her modernity, Cousin Harriet, longing for the
moment when she can read the *Boston Evening Tran-
script*, Mr Apollinax, with his European culture, and his
hostess who listens rather dazed, the housemaids standing

'despondently at area gates' are all 'passing the time' and doing nothing else. The question that Mr Prufrock dare not ask is only superficially the kind of question which one 'pops'. There is another question all the time, which every other question depends on:

> Let us go then, you and I,
> When the evening is spread out against the sky
> Like a patient etherized upon a table;
> Let us go, through certain half-deserted streets,
> The muttering retreats
> Of restless nights in one-night cheap hotels
> And sawdust restaurants with oyster-shells:
> Streets that follow like a tedious argument
> Of insidious intent
> To lead you to an overwhelming question. . . .
> Oh, do not ask, 'What is it?'
> Let us go and make our visit.
>
> In the room the women come and go
> Talking of Michelangelo.

Why not? One must talk of something and Michelangelo is a cultural topic. The absurdity of discussing his giant art, in high-pitched feminine voices, drifting through a drawing-room, adds merely extra irony to the underlying sense of the lines: the escape into any kind of triviality, implied by the phrase: 'Let us go and make our visit.'

The 'sense of the abyss' makes *The Waste Land* essentially different from a great imaginative work in 'the other harmony of prose' which appeared in the same year: James Joyce's *Ulysses*. The two works have much in common. Both are made possible by their authors' absorption of the intellectual developments of the nineteenth and twentieth centuries, and express with imaginative authority what we call the modern mind. The exploration of the past of the human race and of the depths of the human soul, carried out by the anthropologists and the psychologists, appears

not, as in the nineteenth-century poets, in the form of reference to, and discussion of, particular discoveries, but as a
method for the writer to employ for himself: something
that has deeply affected his way of thinking and his manner
of expression. Both works are visions of a city: modern
London and modern Dublin. Both are built upon a famous
myth: *The Waste Land* upon the myth of the mysterious
sickness of the Fisher King in the Grail stories and the blight
of infertility which has fallen upon his lands, which can
only be lifted when the destined Deliverer asks the magic
question or performs the magic act: *Ulysses* upon the myth
of the return of the Wanderer and the cleansing of his home,
and the discovery by the son of his long-lost father and by
the father of his full-grown son. Both combine within a
single work an extraordinary variety of styles, without
destroying a fundamental unity. Both are richly allusive,
and lay their authors open to the charge of pedantry. In
Joyce there is a kind of elephantine pedantry, the pedantry
of a drunken scholar in a Dublin bar, a rhetorical pedantry
that seems to go back to the Middle Ages and the wandering
clerks. In Mr Eliot there is a kind of prim pedantry, the
pedantry of the New England lecture-room, suggesting not
the bar, but the cultured voice and the card-index of the
professor. Both works again juxtapose boldly a modern
world described with the most complete realism, and a world
of romance, epic and high tragedy. But with all these
obvious likenesses the difference between the two works
seems to me to be profound. They display fundamentally
different attitudes to life.

Some critics have claimed that Joyce never escaped from
the influence of his early training, and that he retained always
from his Catholic childhood and youth, after faith had gone,
the need for faith and the sense of sin. I do not think this
is true. I do not find in *Ulysses* either the Christian sense of

sin, or, what is more important, its corollary: the need for salvation by some 'mighty act', beyond man's power to accomplish, something as stupendous as the original act of creation. Joyce is deeply aware of the Christian view of human life. Because he is aware of it he is able to give us in *Ulysses* a deliberate demonstration of what it is like to live without God. But it is a genuine demonstration. He does not in the end uncover a helpless and terrified being confronted with a great darkness. He does not come up against a blank wall. His imagination is not haunted by either the presence or the absence of God. Although he may bore his readers, he seems incapable of boredom himself— perhaps this is why he sometimes wearies those whose appetite for life is less insatiable than his own. And although much that he tells us is horrifying, the effect of his telling us of it is to diminish the horror, not to intensify it. The horror is there as a part of life, and when we look at it steadily it is not so horrible after all. As we read on there seems nothing we need fear or be ashamed of acknowledging in ourselves or in others. The private fantasy, the night terror, the dirty habit, the moral failure, the inner callousness, cease to be shameful. The intolerable thought becomes tolerable. And if there is no feeling of boredom, and the sense of horror fades rather than grows, there is also nothing we can call 'glory'. The glow that lights the last chapter, as Bloom and Stephen talk in Bloom's kitchen, is more friendly and more steady. It neither transforms nor blinds. We could almost invert Mr Eliot's remark, and say of Joyce that he saw beneath 'the boredom and the horror and the glory' both beauty and ugliness. His attitude is not religious but aesthetic.

The difference between *The Waste Land* and *Ulysses* reveals itself if we consider the myths employed and the use made of them. Joyce gives his enormous work coherence by means of plot, and preserves the unities of time and place as well as the unity of action. He takes for his ground plan the *Odyssey*, one of the most shapely and beautifully designed poems in the world. *Ulysses* moves towards a true conclusion, a real solution. The solution is by means of the comic vision; in terms of an adjustment of personalities to the demands of social living. As well as its wonderful incidental comedy, *Ulysses* has the true profundity of comedy, which sees man always in society, and mocks at those who isolate themselves and strain towards the simplifications of tragedy. Mr Eliot discards plot and his poem has no conclusion or solution. He gives his poem unity, partly by means of musical repetition and variation, but mainly by constant references to the underlying myth, and to related myths of death and re-birth. He depends, that is to say, not upon a great work of art in which primitive material has been shaped into a logical design, but upon a myth, which though it has inspired many artists, has never found final and supreme artistic expression. There appears to be something in the Grail legend, as in Arthurian material generally, that resists the ordering of plot. The 'meanings' are always overflowing the narrative and overwhelming the design. But Mr Eliot does not even rely on any one version. He goes back behind any artistic treatment to the bare elements of the myth itself before it was rationalized into a story. He builds his poem on the predicament which the myth embodies, omitting any of the solutions of the predicament which we find in the various Grail stories. *Ulysses*, like the *Odyssey*, moves steadily towards its climax: the homecoming of the hero, and his putting of his house in order. *The Waste Land* moves, if it moves at all, towards some moment which is outside the poem and may never come, which we are still waiting for at the close. It does not so much move towards a solution as make clearer and clearer that a solution is not within our power. We can only wait for the rain to fall.

While in *Ulysses* the three main persons become more and more solid against the background of the crowded city, in *The Waste Land*, though it is thronged with people and we hear many and varied voices, there are no characters in the strict sense, no persons, and in the end the city itself dissolves. In a note Mr Eliot said that the most important personage in the poem, although 'a mere spectator and not indeed a "character" ' was Tiresias: 'Just as the one-eyed merchant, seller of currants, melts into the Phoenician Sailor, and the latter is not wholly distinct from Ferdinand Prince of Naples, so all the women are one woman, and the two sexes meet in Tiresias.' In the same way the time is all time and no time. Though we are plainly at times in modern London, it is an 'unreal city' and in the last section the city has vanished. It is all humanity that seems to be waiting then; the disciples have buried their Lord and the women are lamenting the death of Syrian Adonis or Phrygian Attis. Travellers are making their way through deserts, or to the Southern Pole, or to the village of Emmaus, or to the Chapel Perilous in the mountains, through a landscape peopled with shapes of horror, which fades into the vast Indian plains. Great crowds swarm from ruined cities, the refugees from every empire that has ever fallen. Although *The Waste Land* may begin with the 'dilemma of the modern mind', it discovers that the modern dilemma is the historic dilemma; and to limit the poem's meaning to being primarily the expression of modern lack of faith is to mistake its form and scope. Its true subject is ageless; it discovers a radical defect in human life and makes clear the 'insufficiency of human enjoyments'[1]. Its contrasts in style and its historic

---

[1] See Imlac's disquisition on the Great Pyramid in *Rasselas*: 'I consider this mighty structure as a monument of the insufficiency of human enjoyments. A

references are used to demonstrate that beneath both beauty and ugliness there lurks in all classes and in all ages boredom and terror; all wars are the same war, all love-making is the same love-making, all homecomings the same homecoming:

> And I Tiresias have foresuffered all
> Enacted on this same divan or bed.

The Waste Land is a series of visions: it has neither plot nor hero. The protagonist, or poet, is not a person. Sometimes he is a silent listener, sometimes a voice that asks questions, but gives no answers or only cryptic ones:

> 'What are you thinking of? What thinking? What?
> 'I never know what you are thinking. Think.'
>
> I think we are in rats' alley
> Where the dead men lost their bones.
>
> 'What is that noise?'
>   The wind under the door.
> 'What is that noise now? What is the wind doing?'
>   Nothing again nothing.
>
>   'Do
> 'You know nothing? Do you see nothing? Do you remember
> 'Nothing?'
>
>   I remember
> Those are pearls that were his eyes.

At first we are at least aware of someone, of a silent partner to a conversation in a Munich café, of a man with a girl on a damp evening, of a figure in a lady's bedroom; but this shadowy person becomes a voice that laments by the waters of Lake Leman, the fisherman, Tiresias; and at the end time

king whose power is unlimited, and whose treasures surmount all real and imaginary wants, is compelled to solace, by the erection of a Pyramid, the satiety of dominion and tastelessness of pleasures, and to amuse the tediousness of declining life, by seeing thousands labouring without end, and one stone, for no purpose, laid upon another.'

and place have disappeared. The single figure of the fisher-man with the arid plain behind him is a type of all humanity waiting for the rain to fall, for the fertilizing showers, which may be floods and great waters, whose prelude is lightning, black clouds and thunder.

In the opening movement of *The Waste Land*, which is called 'The Burial of the Dead', we are given a series of contrasted scenes. The common note in all these scenes is fear; the contrasts arise from the various attitudes towards fear. The theme is first stated in the famous opening lines, the comment on the cruelty of spring-time, the pain of new life stirring after the torpor of winter, and we pass to a reminiscence of summer coming with a shower of rain, and then sunlight and an hour of casual talk in the Hofgarten at Munich. The woman who is talking recalls a moment of her childhood, in the mountains, a moment of terror and abandonment to terror:

> He said, Marie,
> Marie, hold on tight. And down we went.

In parenthesis almost, she murmurs: 'In the mountains, there you feel free', before she gives herself away by her summary of the routine of her life now:

> I read, much of the night, and go south in winter.[1]

In violent contrast to this conversational revelation of a routine by which terror is evaded comes the prophetic passage, with its memory of Ezekiel's vision of the valley of dry bones, and the prophetic insistence: 'Come in under the shadow of this red rock.' The image is purposely vague

---

[1] The line can be expanded from the conversation of Ivy and Violet at the beginning of *The Family Reunion*, where Violet with some malice replies to Ivy's envy of those who can afford to follow the sun:
> Go south! to the English circulating libraries,
> To the military widows and the English chaplains,
> To the chilly deck-chair and the strong cold tea—
> The strong cold stewed bad Indian tea.

and terrifying. We may be reminded of Isaiah's vision: 'A man shall be as an hiding place from the wind, and a covert from the tempest; as rivers of water in a dry place, as the shadow of a great rock in a weary land'; but the rock here looms menacing and red, and in its deep shadow there is no comfort, but the terror of our mortality.[1] The prophetic voice declares that we cannot tell what life if any may be stirring in the valley of desolation; we must leave the glare of the sun, the heap of broken images and all the paraphernalia of our life and enter the shadow to see 'fear in a handful of dust'. The lovely passage that follows, set between the sailor's song and the watcher's cry from *Tristan und Isolde*, holds another kind of terror, the terror in the moment of ecstasy in love, when love passes beyond its object, and seems for a moment held in a kind of silence that seems outside time.[2] The girl with the hyacinths is forgotten by her lover, who stands before her silent, rapt by another vision than the vision of her beauty, and with another smell in his nostrils than the smell of rain and flowers. Blind and dumb he looks into 'the heart of light, the silence', and comes back to the world with the cry in his ears of the watcher who tells Tristan that the sea is empty. We are immediately transferred to the parlour of Madame Sosostris, snuffling through her cold, where the fear is fear of the future, the unknown. Her clients look for warnings against future dangers. From her parlour we pass to the crowds flowing over London Bridge on the way to work,

[1] Compare: 'Enter into the rock, and hide thee in the dust, for fear of the Lord, and for the glory of his majesty.' *Isaiah*, ii, 10.
[2] This kind of experience is touched on ironically in the famous 'Whispers of Immortality'. Nice comfortable Grishkin, even while bestowing 'pneumatic bliss', is circumambulated by the Abstract Entities. In the earlier poem we are told that

No contact possible to flesh
Allayed the fever of the bone;

here in a moment of ecstatic recognition of beauty, the mind is suddenly confronted with emptiness and silence.

slaves of time, each with his eyes fixed before his feet, watching the next step only, till the poet recognizing one figure calls to him and halts the procession with a terrifying question and ironic advice:

> That corpse you planted last year in your garden,
> Has it begun to sprout? Will it bloom this year?
> Or has the sudden frost disturbed its bed?
> Oh keep the Dog far hence, that's friend to men,
> Or with his nails he'll dig it up again!

This is the climax of the movement, when the crowds flowing over the bridge are brought to a standstill. It is as if the people walking round in a ring whom Madame Sosostris saw had been interrupted; perhaps by the one-eyed merchant showing what he carries on his back, or by the Hanged Man whom she did not find; or as if the lady who reads much of the night had laid down her book and looked out into the darkness. There is horror in the thought of the corpse buried in the garden, which, while we try to forget it, is taking new shapes beneath the earth; and in the thought of the Dog, which is not mitigated by the copy-book phrase that he is 'friend to men'. The Psalmist's cry 'Deliver my soul from the sword, my darling from the power of the Dog' blends with a familiar image of a dog in a back-garden digging up, and bringing with friendly eagerness, to lay at his master's feet, something he had hoped he had disposed of. The feeling is very complex; we recoil in horror from the thought of the Dog, and in disgust from what the dog in the garden scratches up and brings us; but he is 'friend to men' perhaps even in his manifestation as the Dog, as much as when he lays at our feet some disgusting half-decayed object, wagging his tail with pleasure at his own cleverness.[1]

---

[1] Professor Cleanth Brooks has written: 'I am inclined to take the Dog (the capital letter is Eliot's) as Humanitarianism and the related philosophies

In the second movement 'A Game of Chess' there are only two scenes, and each is very vividly presented.[1] The contrast is in style and setting. The lady's bedroom is described with an extraordinary mingling in the language of admiration and distaste. It is all extremely beautiful, and what is more, extremely expensive, and the phrases echo with a difference phrases describing Cleopatra, the enchanting queen; but the room and the lady are viewed with totally disenchanted eyes. The watcher's eye travels round the room, cataloguing and describing with disillusioned clarity. When we hear the woman speak, we are listening to someone driven by panic, trying to goad her silent companion into speech.[2] When the scene shifts to the public-house, where, instead of the wind under the door, there is the insistent voice of the barman, and we hear Lou speaking to Bill and May, we are at one remove from the real story. The pitiful tale of Albert and Lil comes to us in the hard confident tones of Lou, Lil's treacherous friend. It is Lil that matters, however, Lil, whose husband 'can't bear to look at her', who looks 'so antique' at thirty-one, and who appears to have spent the money Albert gave her for a set of teeth on pills at the chemist, to avoid the consequences of Albert's last leave. Lil has not got 'nerves'; she is merely worn out by poverty and child-bearing and wants Albert to 'leave her alone'. It is the common tragedy of the work-

which in their concern for man extirpate the supernatural—dig up the corpse of the buried god and thus prevent the rebirth of life.' I feel the strongest disinclination to 'take the Dog', with or without capital, in any such way. Such abstractions belong to another way of thinking and are out of place here. The words Humanism and Humanitarianism are in need of a long rest in critical circles.

[1] For the title Mr Eliot refers us to Middleton's *Women Beware Women*, the scene where Livia acting as procuress to the Duke plays chess with the old mother, while her son's wife is being seduced. Perhaps Livia's sardonic comment: 'I've given thee blind mate twice', best sums up the movement.

[2] The man may be either lover or husband, more probably the latter, as then the contrast with the broken marriage of Lil and Albert is the stronger.

ing-class girl, who turns into the prematurely old wife and mother, with only spirit enough left to resent her husband looking elsewhere for what she can no longer give him.[1] Lou's pose of disinterested friend is highly unconvincing, and no doubt Albert, the returned warrior who 'wants a good time', will find some pleasure with her for a while. The first half of the movement shows us a relation that has ceased to enchant; the second a marriage that has collapsed, with an angry baffled husband on one side, and on the other a sullen worn-out wife. The common theme is sterility, or—to use the metaphor from chess—stalemate.

Although it would not be true to say that the third movement, the poem's core, 'The Fire Sermon', shows a way out of this world of loveless loving, it yet presents that world with a new depth. The theme takes a turn. The myth emerges with the figure of the fisherman, and the modern world begins to be merged with other, older worlds. The figures of Tiresias and the coiling serpents are superimposed upon the typist and her young man, Elizabeth and Leicester, and the girl in her canoe and her sisters. There are also moments when we catch a glimpse of another kind of life. We hear children's voices far away beneath the dome; and the 'pleasant whining of a mandoline' above the clatter and chatter of the fishermen lounging in friendly indolence. Something remotely beautiful and solemn is hinted at in the 'inexplicable splendour of Ionian white and gold', and at the close we are aware of a world of purgation: 'burning burning burning burning'. There is also a difference between the boredom and indifference of the typist and her visitor, and the barren flirtation of Elizabeth and Leicester,[2] and

---

[1] The truism of sociologists that working-class women age very quickly was made vividly apparent by the war-time registration of women. It was a shock to see the class distinction in one's own age group expressed as a difference in apparent age in a way it was not in the parallel queues of men.

[2] Some critics have taken the Elizabeth and Leicester passage as affording

the mood in the three quatrains of the Thames-daughters.
The girl in the canoe knows that she is 'undone'; the girl
who paces the pavement at Moorgate, treading on her own
heart, has, in more senses than one, 'lost her self-respect',
and the girl who sits on Margate sands, sits among the
humble 'expecting nothing'. In the first movement we
alternate between routine and fear; in this movement the
alternation is between indifference and horror:

> She turns and looks a moment in the glass,
> Hardly aware of her departed lover;
> Her brain allows one half-formed thought to pass:
> 'Well now that's done: and I'm glad it's over.'

and

> 'On Margate Sands.
> I can connect
> Nothing with nothing.
> The broken finger-nails of dirty hands.
> My people humble people who expect
> Nothing.'

After the lyrical fourth movement 'Death by Water',
with its suggestion of an ineffable peace, a passage backward
through a dream, to a dreamless sleep in which the stain of
living is washed away, the final movement recurs to the
themes of the first. There are again surging crowds as well
as separate figures. The opening speaks again, though in
different terms, of spring, or the moment before spring.
The mountains where the childish Marie had her moment
of ecstatic fear, and which she thinks of nostalgically as a
place where one feels free, are merged with the images of
rock and desert in a landscape of horror and drought. After

---

a contrast of love in the grand style to sordid modern 'affairs'. This is surely
not the point. Of all the lovers of history these are the most preposterous:
Elizabeth, the Virgin Queen, flirting with the astute and ambitious courtier.
When she heard of the birth of James, Elizabeth exclaimed in rage: 'The
Queen of Scots hath a fair son, while I am but a barren stock.' She and
Leicester are playing 'the love game' with every splendid accessory, but the
historic pageantry does not make their relation any the less a barren one.

a momentary vision, which may be the illusion of exhaustion, or may be supreme reality, we enter a region of nightmare and delirium, outside time, and emerge at last on the great plains by the sunken river to hear the thunder speak. Its message is interpreted to us by three symbolic moments: a moment of surrender, a moment of release, and a moment of mysterious well-being. In the first there is an act of the will, accepting, not refusing, abandoning its resistance. In the second a liberating act is performed from without; the prisoner knows himself free. In the third there is a union of power from without and acceptance from within; with effortless ease the heart responds to controlling hands. These three moments are all we are given to hold to: we return to the arid plain and the single figure on the shore fishing. The Bridge over which the crowd flowed is falling down. There come to mind three phrases: a phrase expressing surrender to pain and terror, a phrase declaring longing for freedom, and a phrase that suggests a total destitution, and a hint of that gaiety that can be felt in utter ruin. With these fragments of other men's wisdom the poet leaves us; he slips behind the mask of the mad Hieronimo, mad for grief and rage at the mystery of his son's death, but consenting to 'plie himself to fruitless Poesy', and write that cryptic tragedy in many tongues, by which he will 'make mad the guilty and appal the free'. Once more the thunder reiterates its impossible commands.

The progress in *The Waste Land*, for there is progress, is not the progress of narrative, movement along a line, the progress of an Odysseus towards his home or of Bunyan's pilgrim from the City of Destruction to the Celestial City; it is like the progress of Langland in *Piers Plowman*—a deeper and deeper exploration of an original scene or theme. In *Piers Plowman*, the greatest visionary poem in English, we begin in the Field of Folk, and we are back there again at the close, though the terms are different, with the coming of Anti-Christ. At the close as at the beginning we have to find Piers Plowman to show us the way to Saint Truth. It might be said of *Piers Plowman* as of *The Waste Land* that the close is darker than the beginning, and earlier critics of Langland spoke of the end of his poem as revealing a 'terrible despair'. In both poems we are not, however, moving in a circle, but on a spiral, up or down: 'the way up is the way down'. Throughout we come back continually to the same point at different levels. Like Mr Eliot, Langland gives us vivid pictures of contemporary society, and seems at the beginning to be mainly concerned with the social evils of his day. He was indeed regarded until quite recently as primarily a satirist: the poet of the suffering poor, oppressed by the greed of their lay and spiritual lords. The discovery of Langland's true greatness as a poet has been made by this generation, which has learned to read what was earlier regarded as his incoherent and inconsequent allegory, and sees that his true subject is not the social upheavals of medieval England, but the struggle of the human soul to find the way of salvation. Yet though Langland begins and ends on this earth, where the battle is never won and the search never concluded, at the centre of his poem he leaves this world. In his vision of the Harrowing of Hell, he shows us Life and Death in conflict for the prize of the souls in prison. Since Life wins the victory and a great light shines upon the people who sat in darkness, the triumph of Anti-Christ in the world cannot be final. In Langland the 'mighty act' has been accomplished; the impossible has occurred. The Jesus who 'jousted with the fiend at Jerusalem' won there for ever 'the fruit of Piers Plowman'. He will come again

> as a kynge crouned with angeles
> And han out of helle alle mennes soules.

R. W. Chambers commented on the end of *Piers Plowman*: 'We fail to follow Langland's thought if like John Richard Green and many after him we speak of the poet's "terrible despair". On the contrary, as Dr Coulton has truly said, Langland in his conclusion is "invincible in his faith, since the breakdown of outer bulwarks drives him only to more direct communion with the mystic message which speaks straight to his own heart, and which he can no more disbelieve than he can disbelieve his own existence".' But Langland's faith is not only in the mystic message in his own heart; it is in an event, whose truth his heart confirms. At the centre of his poem there is a revelation of Power, Wisdom and Love in union, redeeming the world, past, present, and to come. *The Waste Land* contains no such revelation. It discovers in its visions man's incapacity to achieve satisfaction, the boredom of his quotidian existence, and the horror of his ignobility. At the centre of its spiral movement there is simply 'the abyss', 'the void' or 'the overwhelming question', the terror of the unknown, which cannot finally be evaded. For all this, its ending is not despair. Stripped of his illusions, his pride broken, man is left to face the final possibility. *The Waste Land* ends with the truth of the human situation as the religious mind conceives it: the beginning of wisdom is fear.

CHAPTER V

THE TIME OF TENSION

Wavering between the profit and the loss
In this brief transit where the dreams cross
The dreamcrossed twilight between birth and dying.
Ash Wednesday

Thou shalt make me hear of joy and gladness: that the bones which thou hast broken may rejoice. *Psalm 51*

ALTHOUGH all Mr Eliot's poetry is the expression of a certain kind of apprehension, the change in his rhythms and style, which has been discussed, and the change in his imagery, is the result of a profound change within this apprehension. In the earlier poetry the apprehension is a kind of glass through which he views the world; it is a dark glass through which life is seen with a strange clarity, but drained of colour and variety. In the poetry that follows *The Waste Land* the apprehension itself becomes more and more the subject. The poet's own image of a shadow can be used to define what is constant and what changes. At the beginning one is aware of life seen in shadow, a grey monotony. The shadow deepens, growing darker and darker, but up to *The Waste Land* the life it darkens is the subject. Now the shadow itself enters the poetry. Where before it was the shadow that was implied, and what we were given was its effect; now the shadow itself is the object of contemplation, and it is the light that casts it that is implied. Paradoxically the acceptance of the shadow lessens the darkness; the darkness of *The Waste Land* becomes a kind of twilight. From within that twilight the poet catches sight of brightness, far off perhaps, but still a brightness which is full of colour. The natural world, which is not looked at directly, has a beauty it did not have in his earlier contemplation of it. Instead of looking out upon the world and seeing sharply defined and various manifestations of the same desolation and emptiness, the poet turns away from the outer world of men to ponder over certain intimate personal experiences. He narrows the range of his vision, withdraws into his own mind, and 'thus devoted, concentrated in purpose' his verse moves 'into another intensity'. The intensity of apprehension in the earlier poetry is replaced by an intensity of meditation.

The withdrawal into the world of inner experience brings with it a new kind of imagery: an imagery deriving from dreams, not from observation, and retaining the inconsequence, the half-understood but deeply felt significance of dreams, their symbolic truth. The new imagery lacks the sharp precision as well as the realism of the earlier. The images are mostly beautiful and poetically suggestive in themselves, whereas the earlier imagery was more often grotesque. They are often drawn from nature, where the most characteristic of the earlier images came from human life lived in cities or, if from nature, from nature in its more sinister aspects. Many of the images are traditional, common symbols which have an age-old meaning: the rose, the garden, the fountain, the desert, the yew. The poet accepts this traditional imagery, and mingles it with images of natural beauty, and with more esoteric images: the white leopards, the jewelled unicorns, the agèd eagle, taken from medieval allegorical fantasy, and the flute-player in blue and green, and the 'silent sister veiled in white and blue', from the world of private myth-making. The figures in *Ash Wednesday* are not persons; they are like figures seen for a moment through the window of a swiftly moving train, where an attitude or a gesture catches our attention and is then gone forever, but remains to haunt the memory. Much

of the imagery has this fleeting vividness; it is not fixed
with the precision of the earlier poetry, and it is only occasionally that the brilliant exact wit of the earlier comparisons
is found:

> the stair was dark,
> Damp, jaggèd, like an old man's mouth drivelling, beyond
> repair,
> Or the toothed gullet of an agèd shark.

This, which has a particular purpose where it occurs, stands
out as alien to the general tone of *Ash Wednesday*, where the
poet seems not to wish to linger on any particular image,
which might by its vividness, aptness, or unexpectedness
interrupt the stream of meditation and distract us from his
essential theme. Many of the images and symbols, unfixed
by precise notation, recur with changing values and changing emphasis.

This recurring imagery, so suggestive, vague and poetic,
when it is contrasted with the intensely particular, sharp
and definite images of the earlier poetry, so traditional and
archetypal in comparison with the realistic and highly
original imagery of the first three volumes, expresses itself
in new rhythms and a new style. Mr Eliot's most striking
quality in the poetry that culminates in *The Waste Land* was
an extreme power of condensation. Whether in free rhymed
verse, or in quatrains, or in the blank verse of 'Gerontion'
his poetry had a peculiar force of expression; it was economi-
cal of words, omitting the merely connecting phrase, ellipti-
cal and in the best sense rhetorical. The new style of *Ash
Wednesday* shows an extraordinary relaxation; it is highly
repetitive, and much of the repetition has an incantatory
effect. It circles round and round certain phrases: 'Because
I do not hope' or 'Teach us to care and not to care'; but it
also plays with words, repeating them, where repetition is
grammatically unnecessary:

> Because these wings are no longer wings to fly
> But merely vans to beat the air
> The air which is now thoroughly small and dry
> Smaller and dryer than the will
> Teach us to care and not to care
> Teach us to sit still.

To make a prose paraphrase of the earlier poetry one would have to expand, as one normally has to expand in paraphrasing poetry; here and in many places in *Ash Wednesday* one would have to condense. The poetic effect of this, and of passages such as the opening of section V, is very curious; it is as if the poet were not thinking of what he is saying. The constant internal assonance and internal rhyme have something of the same effect; they do not appear as if they were consciously meant. The poet's words seem to follow the laws of association rather than those of ratiocination.

> Will the veiled sister pray for
> Those who walk in darkness, who chose thee and oppose thee,
> Those who are torn on the horn between season and season,
> time and time, between
> Hour and hour, word and word, power and power, those who
> wait
> In darkness? Will the veiled sister pray
> For children at the gate
> Who will not go away and cannot pray:
> Pray for those who chose and oppose.

This style is the exact opposite of a rhetorical style, where we are delighted by our perception of the poet's exact placing of each word to give it its maximum force; where we are aware of the rightness of each word, and where sound and rhythm support and underline the sense. It is also wholly undramatic. Point is submerged in a musically flowing rhythm. It is a lyrical style, and in *Ash Wednesday* Mr Eliot reaches what he rarely attained before, the peculiar poignancy of lyric utterance. This lyrical note is sustained with particular beauty in the second and last sections but it is present throughout. The traditional symbols of fountains, springs, rocks, birds, flutes, belong to the world of lyric poetry, where feeling seizes on the first image that comes to the mind, and, not searching for the particular, finds itself employing stock images. Much of the poetry in *Ash Wednesday* reads as if it had simply come to the poet. One is hardly aware of the artist in control of his experience and shaping it into expression.

The change in Mr Eliot's poetry cannot be discussed without reference to the fact that the author of *Ash Wednesday* is a Christian while the author of *The Waste Land* was not. Nobody can underrate the momentousness for any mature person of acceptance of all that membership of the Christian Church entails. But the connection between his acceptance of the Christian Faith, and entry into the communion of the Church, and this change in the content and style of his poetry is a very complex one. Behind any such act of choice and affirmation of belief lie obscure experiences which the conscious mind has translated into intellectual formulas and the conscious will has translated into a decisive step. It is in these obscurer regions that the change in the poetry has its origins, not in the conscious act which is equally a result. Any such act, which makes an apparent break with the past, is itself the result of the past, and when it occurs makes the past assume a pattern not visible before. What is found is what was looked for, and since to look for anything is to act on the hypothesis that it exists, faith precedes faith in a regressive series. But the finding, the recognition of the assumption we have been acting on, which makes an alteration of our way of life, and makes imperative the acceptance of certain obligations, is profoundly mysterious. Nobody can explain why what seems at one time unbelievable, whether beautiful and attractive, or terrifying, comes to seem truth itself and the ground and test of all other truths. The Christian only gives the mystery a name when he speaks of grace; and must assent as he thinks of his choice to the words of the Lord: 'Ye have not chosen me but I have chosen you.' To Christian and non-Christian conversion is incomprehensible. This mystery lies behind *Ash Wednesday*, but the poem does not attempt to approach it. The discovery of faith is assumed. *Ash Wednesday*, as its title warns us, is a poem of purgation; it deals with the mortification of the natural man, the effort to conform the will. But the theme of penitence and the aspiration towards holiness, the acceptance of the Church's discipline of self-examination, contrition, confession and satisfaction, is crossed by another theme. It is clear that the poem springs from intimately personal experience, so painful that it can hardly be more than hinted at, and so immediate that it cannot be wholly translated into symbols. There is anguish both at the exhaustion of feeling and at its recrudescence, at loss and at feeling loss, at not desiring and at still desiring. The double theme: of Christian penitence and resolve, and of personal disaster, gives to almost every line a deep ambiguity which it is not the critic's business to remove. While the conscious mind is occupied with the effort to will what is, to be 'whole in the present', the almost unbearable sense of what was troubles its constancy and makes its affirmations and petitions seem ironic. The struggle between the effort to 'construct something upon which to rejoice' and the pain of existence, the distinction between what the poet wishes to wish, and what he does not wish to wish, but still wishes, gives to *Ash Wednesday* its peculiar intensity. The conscious effort of the will expresses itself in formulas; the movements of the mind and heart express themselves in symbols and visions and intense sense-impressions. The experience out of which the effort of the will arose is not itself approached.

The bridge between *The Waste Land* and *Ash Wednesday* is *The Hollow Men*, the last poem in the volume of Collected Poems of 1925. It is both the last poem in the old manner and the first in the new. When it first appeared it seemed very near to 'the bottom of the abyss'; to express in a more personal fashion the desolation of *The Waste Land*. Its final lines have often been quoted as a cry of extreme defeat, an utterance from the 'heart of darkness'. But it contains, fleetingly, the new images which recur again and again in the later poetry, and the final lines may be taken as the first sign of the new theme of rebirth. The whimper with which the poem closes may be that first faint querulous sound which tells us that a child is born, and is alive. It is possible to interpret the poem as the expression of the belief that

> the moment of birth
> Is when we have knowledge of death.

The Hollow Men approaches the mystery which *Ash Wednesday* refuses to approach and which is at the centre of the Quartets, the subject of the third movement of each: the moment of turning, the point where descent becomes ascent. It is so near that moment that it cannot employ the contrasts of style and manner of *The Waste Land* and *Four Quartets*. Though it is composed in the fivefold form, it is without the variety within the movements which suggests to us musical analogies. The five sections here recall the five acts of a drama, the first containing the exposition, the second introducing a complication, the third the climax, the fourth a new complication arising from the climax and the fifth a resolution. But it is an inner drama; *The Hollow Men* is the ghost of a play. It might be called also the ghost of a poem, since all the poetic elements are reduced to their barest essentials. There is little metrical variety, the effect is of a monotone, a chant without variation. The base is the shortest possible line, the line of two stresses, lengthening out into three and occasionally four, but falling back to the monotony of two. The sentence structure is also simplified; there is much repetition and use of simple parallel clauses and apposition. And the vocabulary shows a similar reduction, single words like 'multifoliate' hinting at resources of poetic diction, as the suggestiveness and rhyme of

> There, is a tree swinging
> And voices are
> In the wind's singing

hint at lyrical beauty. In its images the poem seems to contain in epitome both what goes before and what is to come after. The opening image of the guys, with the brilliant macabre comparison of 'rats' feet over broken glass', the scarecrows tossing in the wind of the second section, the bitter compressed metaphor of 'this broken jaw of our lost kingdoms', recalling the 'dead mountain mouth of carious teeth that cannot spit' of *The Waste Land*, and the rewriting of the nursery rhyme, with the prickly pear in place of the mulberry bush, are like samples of the images we find in such profusion in the 'Preludes', 'Gerontion' and *The Waste Land*. But mingled with these there are traditional poetic images: of stars—'a fading star' and 'the perpetual star'—of 'a tree swinging' and voices 'in the wind's singing', and of 'sunlight on a broken column'. These, with the Dantesque 'gathered on this beach of the tumid river', and the unexpected introduction of the religious symbol of the 'multifoliate rose' from *The Divine Comedy*, point forward to the imagery of *Ash Wednesday* and *Four Quartets*. And the use of these images as recurring symbols, and of the potent word 'kingdom' to lead up to the broken petitions from the Lord's Prayer, anticipates the treatment of imagery in the later poems.

The image which dominates the centre of the poem is the image of eyes. The central sections are about being looked at and not being looked at; about eyes that look upon us with reproach or judge us, eyes that seem to smile upon us or look on us with serenity; and about gazing at a stony eyeless face, or groping in a darkness where we neither see nor are seen. This image of eyes, a look imagined, and a look remembered, occurs in a very early poem, written in 1911,[1] the poem which ends the *Prufrock* volume and appears so different from all the other poems collected there, and indeed from anything before *Ash Wednesday*: 'La Figlia Che Piange'. The poem is actually about a statue of a weeping girl, which the poet missed seeing in a museum in Italy,[2] though it is also a poem about parting. The poet imagines the girl, clasping her flowers to her, in the act of turning away, 'with a fugitive resentment in her eyes'. This is how a parting should take place, not clumsily and painfully as it does in life. The contrast between the dream kingdom of the imagination, where life has the style of art, and the reality of human pain seems to underlie the poem, and gives to it a greater poignancy than can be accounted for by its ostensible subject.

A later and deeply moving version of this experience of parting, and of weeping eyes that have turned away, is a poem which is printed among the Minor Poems in *Collected Poems* (1936), and which originally appeared, as the first of 'Doris's Dream Songs' in *The Chapbook* No. 39 (1924).[3]

---

[1] I take the date from the admirable French translation of Mr Eliot's poems by M. Pierre Leyris (*Poèmes* 1910–1930. Paris 1947). Mr John Hayward supplied for this edition the dates for each poem, as well as writing valuable extra notes to *The Waste Land*.

[2] In a talk broadcast in the Third Programme in August 1948, Mr John Hayward said that the emotion expressed in this poem has 'deceived many people into supposing that "The Weeping Girl" must have been a real girl with whom the poet had been in love—a mistake possibly originating in the poem's Latin epigraph: "O quam te memorem virgo". The poem in fact is one of speculation and regret, about a statue which Mr Eliot had looked for in a museum in Italy but had failed to find'.

[3] The third 'song' was used as Part III of *The Hollow Men*.

Eyes that last I saw in tears
Through division
Here in death's dream kingdom
The golden vision reappears
I see the eyes but not the tears
This is my affliction

This is my affliction
Eyes I shall not see again
Eyes of decision
Eyes I shall not see unless
At the door of death's other kingdom
Where, as in this,
The eyes outlast a little while
A little while outlast the tears
And hold us in derision.

In this poem the tormenting memory of an actual parting between two human beings seems implied by the image of eyes. But in *The Family Reunion*, where this image is again central, it has lost its associations with the particular, however much we may feel that the force of the image derives from a particular undisclosed human situation. Dramatic form makes necessary the concrete embodiment of this general sense of being looked at, and Mr Eliot has translated the 'eyes' of the play into the figures of the Eumenides. It would have perhaps been better if he had left these watching and pursuing eyes nameless, for the classical associations rather hinder appreciation of their simple and terrifying significance. The transformation the image undergoes in the play is from the plural to the singular: the eyes which stared and spied become in Harry's mind, at the climax of the recognition scene with Agatha, 'the single eye above the desert'; just as the 'sleepless hunters that will not let me sleep' become 'what waits and wants me, and will not let me fall'. This obsessing image does not appear in *Ash Wednesday*, where it is 'the golden vision' that reappears; not the weeping eyes but the blown hair and the flowers. In

Four Quartets it has disappeared, as if after its development in *The Family Reunion* it had ceased to compel the poet's imagination. It survives only in a parenthesis in *Burnt Norton*, where it has lost all its power to torment: 'the roses had the look of flowers that are looked at'. Here to be looked at seems to imply the happiness of being cared for.

In *The Hollow Men* this image hovers between a natural and a religious significance. The use of the metaphor 'the Eyes of the Lord', the prayer 'Look upon me O Lord', and the phrase 'in Thy sight' makes an equivocal use of the image natural. If the line 'Eyes I dare not meet in dreams' primarily suggests the poignant sense of shame we feel before reproachful human eyes, it is capable of suggesting also the emotion of the Psalmist exclaiming: 'In thy sight may no man living be justified.' At its first use the human significance of the image is uppermost, at its last, the religious, but the fact that it can be used in both ways makes it neither exclusively human at its first use, nor exclusively religious at its last. The hope of empty men is that the eyes may 're-appear', that our human experience may be made valid:

> both a new world
> And the old made explicit, understood
> In the completion of its partial ecstasy,
> The resolution of its partial horror.

The eyes we dare not meet in dreams are, whichever emphasis we give them, eyes of judgment. The look we are aware of makes us feel our own insufficiency, our hollowness; it is a look that finds us out. In Conrad's *Heart of Darkness*, to which the epigraph: 'Mistah Kurtz—he dead', points us, Marlow thinks it was the wilderness that found out Kurtz:

There was something wanting in him—some small matter which, when the pressing need arose, could not be found under his magnificent eloquence. Whether he knew of this deficiency himself I can't say. I think the knowledge came to him at last— only at the very last. But the wilderness had found him out early, and had taken on him a terrible vengeance for the fantastic invasion. I think it had whispered to him things about himself which he did not know, things of which he had no conception till he took counsel with this great solitude—and the whisper had proved irresistibly fascinating. It echoed loudly within him because he was hollow at the core.

But Mr Kurtz's hollowness is of a different kind from the hollowness of the 'pilgrims' with their staves, the exploiters who condemn his 'unsound methods', and it is different from the hollowness of their wretched victims, whose 'moribund shapes', 'scattered in every pose of contorted collapse', like inhabitants of 'the gloomy circle of some Inferno', may have suggested to the poet the image of the lolling guys. For Kurtz, as Marlow insists, was 'a remarkable man', whose dying whisper: 'The horror! The horror!' was at least 'the expression of some sort of belief; it had candour, it had conviction, it had a vibrating note of revolt in its whisper, it had the appalling face of a glimpsed truth.' Marlow, with some sense of shame compares his own experience of imminent death with Kurtz's:

I have wrestled with death. It is the most unexciting contest you can imagine. It takes place in an impalpable grayness, with nothing underfoot, with nothing around, without spectators, without clamour, without glory, without the great desire of victory, without the great fear of defeat, in a sickly atmosphere of tepid scepticism, without much belief in your own right, and still less in that of your adversary. If such is the form of ultimate wisdom, then life is a greater riddle than some of us think it to be. I was within a hair's-breadth of the last opportunity for pronouncement, and I found with humiliation that probably I would have nothing to say. That is the reason why I affirm that Kurtz was a remarkable man. He had something to say. . . . True, he had made that last stride, he had stepped over the edge, while I had been permitted to draw back my hesitating foot. And perhaps in this is the whole difference; perhaps all the wisdom, and all truth, and all sincerity, are just compressed into that inappreciable moment of time in which we step over the threshold of the invisible.

Conrad said of the three stories that make up the volume *Youth* that they presented the three ages of man, and *The Hollow Men*, like *Heart of Darkness* is in part a work that presents the crisis we call middle age. What *Ash Wednesday* calls 'the infirm glory of the positive hour' has passed; it seems only a dream, an illusion under the power of death. The world we inhabit is the 'twilight kingdom', grey and growing darker towards the moment when we must 'step over the threshold of the invisible' and enter 'death's other Kingdom'. But the three kingdoms of death can bear another meaning. The dream kingdom of death may be the world of illusion, of imagination and reverie, free from the pain of actual experience, where the idea is untranslated into reality, the potency not realized in existence, unshadowed and therefore unreal. The twilight kingdom is then this world, 'the dreamcrossed twilight between birth and dying', and those 'who have crossed with direct eyes, to death's other Kingdom' are those who have stepped into the darkness, leaving behind the world of illusion to enter the shadow itself. They have entered a Kingdom 'which is not of this world', which appears as a kingdom of death to those who are 'gathered on this beach of the tumid river'.

At the beginning of the poem there is a feeling of total meaninglessness, the extremity of scepticism which Marlow said he felt on the brink of death: 'a vision of grayness without form filled with physical pain, and a careless contempt for the evanescence of all things—even of this pain itself.' The hollow men are like the wailing figures Dante saw first in the no-man's-land before he crossed the river into Hell, those who 'lived without blame and without praise', whom Hell rejects, for if they were to enter Hell 'the wicked would have some glory over them'. These are they 'who have no hope of death', 'hateful to God and to His enemies', those who were never alive and whom Mercy and Justice alike disdain. In the second section, where the poet speaks in the singular, the origin of this sense of vacuity is given. Here is the refusal itself. There has been both joy and pain. But the joy is a remote and distant idea; when approached it becomes pain, and that pain is intolerable. The vision of happiness translated into actuality has become 'that final meeting in the twilight kingdom', something unendurable even in dreams. Better be a scarecrow, wearing deliberate disguises, responding to any chance gust, aware at times of a visionary sunlight and sweetness, than face the agony of living our dreams. The vision we call love and the reality we know as pain Shelley saw as the bright reflection and the dark shadow of the 'delicate monster' Desolation:

> Ah sister! Desolation is a delicate thing:
>   It walks not on the earth, it floats not on the air,
> But treads with lulling footstep, and fans with silent wing
>   The tender hopes which in their hearts the best and gentlest
>   bear;
> Who, soothed to false repose by the fanning plumes above
>   And the music-stirring motion of its soft and busy feet,
> Dream visions of aëreal joy, and call the monster, Love,
>   And wake, and find the shadow Pain, as he whom now we
>   greet.

This desolation itself is the experience of the third section. In utter loneliness, remote from the vision of joy and the reality of pain, in the dead land, in solitude, the form of desolation itself can be known, and it is desire. The dead in life stretch out their hands, if only to the blind and dumb images they themselves have raised. The question remains unanswered whether over the threshold, waking from the sleep of death, or in the night of the senses, our love and longing find any answer; or whether in death's other kingdom we only deceive ourselves and there is no object for our tenderness but our own broken idols. In the final darkness, where the blind grope together without speech, even desire seems extinguished in the nightmare of abandonment. All that remains is the hope of the hopeless: that in utmost extremity the eyes will reappear, not as a vision that fades as we approach it, nor as a judgment that we cannot endure, but as Mercy and Justice together, the star that does not fade, the unwithering rose of many petals, in which both our joy and pain are gathered. In the closing summary all that is certain is the Shadow, falling between idea and reality, the inevitable accompaniment of temporal life. In face of this riddle of existence we can either return to the scepticism of the opening and let our last word on life be what Marlow calls 'a phrase of careless contempt': 'Life is very long'; or we can by an act of faith assert that there is meaning, though not here in the kingdoms of death, and with the prayer 'Thine is the Kingdom' wait for the eyes' reappearing. The poem ends ambiguously. We may say that it ends with an attempt to pray, or we may say it ends by finding prayer impossible. And the final jingle may be read as a contemptuous epitaph on a world that comes to an end without the splendour and grandeur of catastrophe, but with the simple whimper of defeat, the gasp of exhaustion; or as a riddling answer to the riddle of life, declaring in childish terms that the world ends with the cry of helpless infancy: the whimper of a little creature drawing its first breath.

In *Ash Wednesday* the choice has been made. Choice and decision are not its subject. It is not a single continuous poem, but a group of poems on aspects of a single theme. In religious terms the theme is penitence; and penitence can be defined as a proper attitude to the past, a recognition of the present and a resolve for the future. The rhythms of the poems do not work towards climaxes, nor are effects sought by the use of rhythmic or verbal contrasts. The first three poems originally appeared separately in periodicals and not in the order in which they appear in the volume.[1] This suggests that it is probably a mistake to attempt to trace a development of the theme from poem to poem. There is less a progress of thought than a circling round, and the centre around which this meditative poetry revolves is not an idea or an experience so much as a certain state of mind which is aspired to. The absence of clear structure is the formal equivalent of this peculiarity in the central subject. *Ash Wednesday* stands apart from *The Hollow Men*, *The Waste Land* and *Four Quartets*, which are explorations of experience, in that the experiences which it contains seem marginal to its true subject. The subject is an aspiration to a state which can only be suggested, by experiences drawn from dreams, or by the figures of the Lady and the veiled sister, types of the blessed soul. The aspiration itself is expressed mainly in phrases taken from the classic prayers of Western Christianity, and hardly at all in the poet's own words.

The first poem turns on subtle distinctions between nearly allied conditions: the distinction between regret or remorse and penitence; between indifference and detachment. In this poem the mind is awake, aware of its loss; it knows that power has gone, never to return, and that a once glorious vision has fled forever. It has to learn to balance on the knife-edge between the bitterness of regret and the cynicism of relief. It must forgo the endless recapitulation of the past, accept that what is done cannot be undone, and that what is lost cannot be recovered. Instead

[1] 'Perch'io non spero' (*Commerce* xv, 1928). 'Salutation' (*Saturday Review of Literature* iv, 20, 1927). 'Som de l'Escalina' (*Commerce* xxi, 1929).

of accepting this with tired indifference, it must rejoice

> having to construct something
> Upon which to rejoice.

The poem's intensity comes from the concentration of the will, which prevents either the note of hopeless regret or that of bitter irony becoming dominant. Each is felt, drawing the mind away from its attempt to repose in mercy and judgment, from accepting that 'God is greater than our heart, and knoweth all things'. The opening line: 'Because I do not hope to turn again', repeated and modified, is adapted from the opening line of a poem by Cavalcanti, written when he was dying in exile and had no hope of ever returning to Tuscany and to his lady. In the Italian it has simply the pathos of exile; in Mr Eliot's adaptation it has an altogether grimmer note. It suggests that a capacity for response has now been exhausted, and the phrase seems nearer to Othello's savage mockery of Desdemona's sweet pliability[1] than to the wistfulness of Cavalcanti. The face is set in another direction, knowing that the dead past must bury its dead.

In the second poem we are in the world of vision, but there is the same balance precariously maintained between intense bitterness and heartless levity, caring and not caring. The opening image of the three white leopards, sinister and dangerous, but beautiful beasts, gorged and content with their feast, is not I think susceptible of allegorical interpretation. It should be allowed to remain as a potent and

---

[1] LOD. I do beseech your lordship, call her back.
OTH. Mistress!
DES.　　My lord?
OTH.　　　What would you with her sir?
LOD. Who, I, my lord?
OTH. Ay; you did wish that I would make her turn;
　　Sir, she can turn, and turn, and yet go on,
　　And turn again; and she can weep, sir, weep;
　　And she's obedient, as you say, obedient,
　　Very obedient.

mysterious image. Immobile, satisfied, reposeful, the great beasts sit beneath the tree, their work of devouring done. The bones lie before them white and shining, picked clean, while that which had been contained in the bones chirps like a bird. The image is at once outrageous and curiously beautiful, for there is no feeling of resentment, but rather a feeling of finality. Good, lovely, and remote, withdrawn to contemplation in a white gown, the Lady sits apart. It is because her mind is wholly directed away from the scene that the bones, forgotten, shine with brightness. Inspired by her forgetfulness they aspire to forget. The use of the verb 'dissemble'—which seems to be employed primarily in a special sense as the opposite of 'assemble', to describe a falling apart of those elements that made up the personality, though its usual sense of 'disguised' is still present, since an 'I' lurks here among these scattered fragments—adds a flavour of irony, which is enforced by the slightly grandiose phrases in which the unwanted is 'proffered' to the unwanting. There is again a double sense in the verb 'recovers'. It implies both a covering over again of what has been exposed—those poor inward parts which the leopards have torn out and cast away—and a restoring to life of this residuum.[1] Throughout the poem there is a mingling of personal symbolism with prophetic vision. The thirty-seventh chapter of Ezekiel, where the prophet beheld in vision a valley full of bones 'and lo they were very dry', underlies the main poem, while the visions of Isaiah of the wilderness and solitary places, and of the desert that shall blossom as a rose, provide an undertone to the litany of praise. But these are elements and do not by themselves provide any key to the poem. The command: 'Prophesy

---

[1] This second sense is archaic, but it is established for poets by the conclusion of Drayton's famous sonnet on the death of Love:

Now if thou would'st, when all have given him over,
From death to life thou might'st him yet recover.

unto the wind, prophesy, son of man', is given a quite different turn by the addition of 'to the wind only for only the wind will listen', and the Rose of memory, Rose of forgetfulness, is a far more complex symbol than the rose that the prophet sees blooming with miraculous beauty in the desert places. The exquisite lightness and beauty of the rhythm of the litany which the bones sing to the Lady is their tribute to one who has learned 'to care and not to care' or, in the terms of this poem, to remember and to forget with simplicity. As the Lady is the type of the bones' aspiration, she approximates to Our Lady, in whom is united

> quantunque in creatura è di bontate.

She is felt behind the Lady of Silences, both Virgin and Mother, uniting perfect innocence and supreme experience, at once Mater Gloriosa and Mater Dolorosa, who smiles by the cradle and weeps by the cross, and stands crowned, with the swords piercing her heart. The return to the movement of the opening brings us back to the vision of the bones scattered beneath the juniper tree in the cool of the day. But the leopards have vanished, for here is the end of the torment

> Of love unsatisfied
> The greater torment
> Of love satisfied.

It is the rhythm here as in the opening that preserves from bitterness such a parenthesis as 'we did little good to each other' and allows us to accept simply such a phrase as 'the blessing of sand'. It makes the phrase: 'And neither division nor unity matters' uncynical, and the repetition of: 'This is the land', with the added: 'We have our inheritance', not ironic. It is indeed in the rhythms of the poem that its meaning is felt, for in the rhythm can be heard that ripple which can be heard again in the central movement of *Little Gidding*, where, though the diction and the images are so different, the theme is also

> the use of memory:
> For liberation—not less of love but expanding
> Of love beyond desire, and so liberation
> From the future as well as the past.

It is this supple, flowing rhythm that gives to disenchanted phrase and disenchanted scene a kind of enchantment. The music holds the promise of peace, and of more than peace, of joy.

With the third poem we have left the world of vision for the world of allegory and exact symbolism. The image of stairs is traditional and obvious, and the three temptations are vivid and unambiguous. The struggle with the devil of the stairs

> who wears
> The deceitful face of hope and of despair,

takes us back to the matters we 'too much discuss too much explain'. The twisting and turning of shape and devil

> Under the vapour in the fetid air

is a wonderful realization of the misery and oppression that accompany interminable internal debate, the stale taste and headache that this kind of debauch brings. Beyond this lies the darkness of sheer self-disgust, the sense of decay and failure, when everything seems without meaning, not strange and terrifying but only sordid and disgusting. Round the turn of the next stair, emerging from this darkness, the world suddenly appears, as through a window, entrancingly beautiful. The movement of the verse as the lines lengthen out makes us feel how powerful is this revival of the natural man and of the capacity for joy; how sweet and fresh the world appears. Distracted for a moment in its ascent the mind lapses into a momentary dream, until it recollects its task and in the presence of that recollection the scene fades. These successive moods, or well-known psychological states, we can call the temptations to self-absorption, self-disgust and self-indulgence; or we can see them as the hindrances to sincerity, contrition and love. Mrs Duncan-Jones, in an essay on *Ash Wednesday*[1] connects the three stairs not with the ascent of the purgatorial mount in *The Divine Comedy* but with the three steps that lead to the mount, which Dante's commentators interpret allegorically as sincerity, contrition and love, and anagogically as contrition, confession and expiation by the blood of Christ. The most Dantesque of the six poems in its narrative pattern and in the sharpness of its images, this poem can be interpreted on three levels, the psychological, the moral and the spiritual. The three meanings are all valid in isolation from each other, in a manner in which the various meanings in the visionary second poem are not. In the poetry of vision the different levels of meaning cannot be distinguished, and an interpretation in one set of terms is not simply partial but positively false.

Although *Ash Wednesday* does not seem designed to present a development, yet there is a break after the third poem, and the tension seems to slacken. The last three poems are more closely linked to each other in imagery and style than are the first three, and there is a continuity of thought between them. The veiled nun-like figure who in the fourth poem appears at the climax and makes a mysterious sign, who is prayed to in the fifth poem as an intercessor for those torn by doubt and indecision, and invoked in the last poem as 'Blessèd sister, holy mother', is a gentler figure than the Lady of Silences. Her gesture seems to be one of assent, or approval, or even of blessing; it releases the waters of

[1] In *T. S. Eliot: A Study of his Writings by Several Hands*, ed. B. Rajan.

the fountain and is answered by the song of the bird, repeating the words the poet has heard echoing in his dreams: 'Redeem the time, redeem the dream.' Like the Lady of Silences she also in her virtue points us to Our Lady, but particularly to Our Lady of the Annunciation, who made assent to the message of the angel and bore for mankind the Eternal Word. The spiritual centre of these last three poems is the Incarnation, by which all time is redeemed. The mystery they expound is the mystery of the prologue to St John's Gospel: 'He was in the world, and the world was made by him, and the world knew him not. He came unto his own, and his own received him not.'

The fourth poem returns to the thought of memory. It recalls a springtime of woodland flowers and varied green, and a summer brilliant but not fierce, made lovely by a beloved presence. The years that have borne away 'the fiddles and the flutes' restore in dreams the beauty of that earlier time. Mysteriously folded in white light, sheathed in brightness as a flower is in its leaves, the beloved figure moves again. As in an allegorical pageant, youth and love are borne away to burial in a gilded car drawn by jewelled unicorns, and the cry is heard echoing:

> Redeem
> The time. Redeem
> The unread vision in the higher dream.

The gentle admonitory figure of the silent sister, veiled in white and blue, the colours of the earlier presence, is seen standing behind the garden god, the genius of fertility, whose flute is silent now. Both memory and dream are gracious and the dream seems to hallow the memory. Both are tokens of 'the word unheard, unspoken', moments in which an exile seems to breathe the air of home. If this poem seems to hint at the words 'He was in the world', the next expands the words 'and the world knew him not'. There is no dream or vision here, only a sense of time lost and time misspent, of choice made and retracted, of decision that is never decisive. The dogmatic affirmation of the mystery of the Logos, changeless and constant, and the solemn refrain from the Reproaches contrast with the questionings of those who walk in darkness, who choose and oppose, affirm and deny, and even at the last find a desert in the garden, a garden in the desert of drouth; discovering in the mouth, savourless and withered, some last remnant of the old garden sin. The veiled sister, type of the surrendered soul, is implored by those who are torn and divided. She redeems the time in silence, keeping all things and pondering them in her heart. They are whirled by the unstilled world, at the mercy of the season and the hour, wavering to the last; and even at the last impelled only by disgust at what was once sweet and is now tasteless, hard and dry, but has still to be renounced. Beyond this inconclusive effort there is simply the patience of God, which endures the treachery of men, and the beauty of holiness which can make intercession for it. In the last poem, on the other hand, there is an acceptance of natural human weakness. The extraordinary lyrical beauty with which the revival of the senses and of the desire of the heart is expressed is untroubled by remorse or a sense of shame. Though the heart is wavering and inconstant, the will is set. It is content to wait in 'the time of tension between dying and birth' in a place of solitude crossed by dreams—the dreams of innocent human happiness, of human love, and of sanctity—between the two yews, whispering of death and of life. The blessed sister, holy mother, who is invoked to keep the will true and the heart sincere, as exemplar of patience and love, is also the spirit of the fountain and of the garden, of the river and the sea. There is in this poem a feeling of the goodness of creation: that 'the world was made by him'.

Ash Wednesday is the most obscure of Mr Eliot's poems, and the most at the mercy of the temperament and beliefs of the individual reader. It has not the formal beauty of *The Waste Land* and *Four Quartets*, but the haunting and disturbing beauty of those works in which one is too conscious of the author's presence. We are teased by a curiosity we do not feel where there is a more complete separation between 'the man who suffers and the mind which creates'. For though the author speaks in his own person, without the use of a 'persona' such as Gerontion, or the various masks which the poet of *The Waste Land* adopts, he is not speaking to us. The symbols and images he employs have the arbitrariness of the individual's inner world, and have hardly emerged into the self-explanatory world of art. The speaker is not wholly willing to share his secret, perhaps because it is still in part a secret from himself.

By contrast, the four Ariel poems, which are exactly contemporary with *Ash Wednesday*, are simplicity itself. These short pieces seem to be inspired by two connected impulses: the impulse to treat with strict objectivity aspects of the theme of *Ash Wednesday*, and the impulse to write for a larger and more miscellaneous audience. All four were first published separately in cheap booklet form and had a wide circulation. The first two are monologues put into the mouths of historic personages, who have witnessed an historic event.[1] Each has a clear literary source. *The Journey of the Magi* (1927) is based on a sermon preached before King James at Whitehall in 1622 by Lancelot Andrewes. Its opening lines are taken directly from the sermon and the whole poem owes much to the rhythms of Andrewes's prose, with its colloquial vividness, its wrestling with words and

---

[1] I beg the question of the historicity of the New Testament deliberately, since it must be assumed in reading these poems, which have the objectivity of imaginative historical reconstruction.

meanings, and its staccato movement. *A Song for Simeon* (1928) elaborates the *Nunc Dimittis* and the prophecy of Simeon in the second chapter of St Luke's Gospel, and it echoes the parallelisms and the cadences of the Authorized Version. Both poems have a straightforward clarity, and employ a firm sentence structure which allows of conventional punctuation. The third poem, *Animula* (1929), is a generalized meditation with particular examples on the course of human life between its issuing from the hand of God and its issuing from the hand of Time. It has a lucid impersonality. The last of the poems, *Marina* (1930), the most beautiful, returns to the use of myth. The monologue here is spoken by the old King Pericles, at the climax of his awakening, finding after storm and tempest and a long voyage his daughter Marina, lost at sea and restored by the sea. The theme of restoration is perfectly translated into the terms of the myth. The beautiful natural imagery of *Ash Wednesday* is here at the heart of the poem. Its subject is the hope of *The Hollow Men*; the 'eyes re-appear', the 'images return'.

In *The Journey of the Magi* and *A Song for Simeon* the speakers are both old men. The event to which they are witnesses marks the end of an old dispensation and the beginning of a new. It has made the old dispensation impossible and overturned the values by which they had lived. Both poems are poems of crisis, in which the new seems destructive of the old. The old king has returned to his kingdom and feels his people, clutching their gods who were once his gods, are alien to him. He waits impatiently for the release of bodily death. Simeon, a 'just and devout' man, recalls his life lived in obedience to the law and in honour, and sees in vision the coming destruction of Jerusalem and the Temple, the dispersion of his people, and the disappearance of all that he has lived by. He sees the glory and derision to be earned by those who will bear the scandal of the cross, 'to the Jews a stumbling block and to the Greeks foolishness'. He knows there is an ecstasy of thought and prayer for those called into the new Israel of the Church, and he knows it is not for him, for he belongs to the world of the Old Covenant. 'Prosperity is the blessing of the Old Testament; adversity is the blessing of the New.'

Bishop Andrewes's sermon supplies the two basic ideas of *The Journey of the Magi*. In expanding the text: 'Behold there came wise men from the East', Andrewes dwells first on the faith of the wise men, who braved the pains and perils of such a long journey at such a time of year. 'First, the distance of the place they came from. It was not hard by as the shepherds—but a step to Bethlehem over the fields; this was riding many a hundred miles, and cost them many a day's journey. . . . This was nothing pleasant, for through deserts, all the way waste and desolate. Nor easy neither; for over the rocks and crags of both Arabias, specially Petraea their journey lay. . . . Exceeding dangerous, as lying through the midst of the "black tents of Kedar", a nation of thieves and cut-throats; to pass over the hills of robbers, infamous then, and infamous to this day. . . . It was no summer progress. A cold coming they had of it at this time of the year, just the worst time of the year to take a journey, and specially a long journey in. The ways deep, the weather sharp, the days short, the sun farthest off *in solstitio brumali*, "the very dead of winter".' Later Andrewes asks what they found. He compares them with the Queen of Sheba who also came from afar but saw Solomon in all his glory. 'Weigh what she found, and what these here—as poor and unlikely a birth as could be, ever to prove a King, or any great matter. No sight to comfort them, nor a word for which they any whit the wiser; nothing worth their travel. . . . Well, they will take Him as they find Him, and all this notwithstanding, worship Him for all that.' Mr Eliot has added to these two ideas of the long journey and the mysterious obscurity of the event they had travelled so far to see his own characteristic theme of the pain of birth, his conception of birth as a kind of death; but he has strictly subordinated his personal theme and his personal imagery to the quasi-dramatic nature of his poem. In the beautiful passage on the 'temperate valley' the images, whatever private significance they may have for the poet, are given general significance by their prophetic pointing to Calvary. The three trees on the low sky are portents of the trees to be lifted upon the hill outside the city wall of Jerusalem, and the six hands dicing for pieces of silver foretell both the dicing at the foot of the cross and the price of innocent blood.[1] The whole scene is thus not only an interlude on the journey, but an image of the carelessness and cruelty of the world into which the child is born.

If *The Journey of the Magi* and *A Song for Simeon* treat in isolation the exhaustion of spirit which is one element in *Ash Wednesday*, *Marina* embodies what *Ash Wednesday* only

---

[1] In *The Use of Poetry*, speaking of an author's imagery, Mr Eliot says: 'It comes from the whole of his sensitive life since early childhood. Why, for all of us, out of all that we have heard, seen, felt, in a lifetime, do certain images recur, charged with emotion, rather than others? The song of one bird, the leap of one fish, at a particular place and time, the scent of one flower, an old woman on a German mountain path, six ruffians seen through an open window playing cards at night at a small French railway junction where there was a water-mill: such memories may have symbolic value, but of what we cannot tell, for they come to represent depths of feeling into which we cannot peer.' The transformation of this personal memory to give it general symbolic significance is an example in little of the whole poem's translation of personal experience into the terms of a familiar story.

> Then at dawn we came down to a temperate valley,
> Wet, below the snow line, smelling of vegetation;
> With a running stream and a water-mill beating the darkness,
> And three trees on the low sky,
> And an old white horse galloped away in the meadow.
> Then we came to a tavern with vine-leaves over the lintel,
> Six hands at an open door dicing for pieces of silver,
> And feet kicking the empty wine-skins.

hints at. The dream which is there only a dream is here the reality to which a sleeper wakes.

> And approach to the meaning restores the experience
> In a different form, beyond any meaning
> We can assign to happiness.

The labour of the building of the boat is now remembered and forgotten. For all its unseaworthiness it has made the voyage. The call of the bird, the scent of the pine, coming through the dissolving fog, the whispers heard in sleep, the face 'less clear and clearer' and the fluctuation of the pulse beating 'less strong and stronger' are the prelude to a moment of ecstatic recognition. As *The Hollow Men* is the bridge between *The Waste Land* and *Ash Wednesday*, *Marina* is the bridge between *Ash Wednesday* and *Four Quartets*. What *Ash Wednesday* cannot express directly is here expressed, without the aid of specifically Christian phrase or symbol. But the whole poem is penetrated with the Christian hope, the fulfilment of the promise 'Behold I make all things new'. At the close of *The Waste Land* the image of the open sea and a boat moving on it easily and gaily is used as an image of beatitude. It is a wonderful image of that inward peace and calm to which the great religions of the East aspire. The voyage in *Marina* discovers in the ocean an island, and sees again a beloved face. Its theme is not the immortality of the soul, but resurrection.

CHAPTER VI

THE LANGUAGE OF DRAMA

I gotta use words when I talk to you
But if you understand or if you don't
That's nothing to me and nothing to you.
Sweeney in Sweeney Agonistes

Those who do not do the same
How should they know what I do?
How should you know what I do? Yet how much more
Should you know than these madmen beating on the door.
Thomas in Murder in the Cathedral

I can only speak
And you cannot hear me. I can only speak
So you may not think I conceal an explanation,
And to tell you that I would have liked to explain.
Harry in The Family Reunion

MR ELIOT'S attempts to render his vision of the boredom, the horror and the glory of life in dramatic terms have given us the finest dramatic verse that has been written in English since the seventeenth century. The question that is debateable is whether he has yet succeeded in writing a great play. The question does not arise because we are disturbed by faults in the mechanics of play-writing: clumsiness in exposition, insufficient or improbable motivation, too obvious dependence on coincidence—the kind of complaint that is often brought against the poet who attempts to write for the stage. These things can be ignored if our imaginations are deeply enough stirred by the dramatic and poetic power with which the main situation is expressed. The problem of Mr Eliot's plays arises at their dramatic centre. Their defect, if it is a defect, is a fundamental one; their success, if it is a success, makes it necessary to define again what we mean by drama. We have to ask whether dramatic expressiveness has been achieved if, at the climax of a play, the hero cannot express himself either in action or in words, and the bystander who has the clearest insight can only tell us that what has happened is inexplicable in this world, 'the resolution is in another'. Mr Eliot's plays are full of dramatic moments and of dramatic poetry; but dramatic moments and dramatic verse do not necessarily add up to a drama. One wonders whether the central subject has been conceived dramatically, and indeed whether it is susceptible of dramatic treatment at all. Could Mr Eliot say of the martyrdom of Thomas Becket or the conversion of Harry what Henry James said of the subject of 'The Reverberator'? James said of his story that it might be denied the grace of anecdote, because anecdote raised always the question: 'Who is it about?' But he thought his story had dramatic logic: 'I felt my subject for all its slightness as a small straight *action*, and so placed it in that blest drama light, which really making for intelligibility as nothing else does, orders and regulates, even when but faintly turned on.' It is this 'blest drama light', making for intelligibility, which seems to be lacking in both *Murder in the Cathedral* and *The Family Reunion*. One goes out from the theatre, after a performance of either, having been deeply interested and even deeply moved. But one has not been interested by either dramatic action or dramatic personality. What has happened has not affected us, and the characters to whom it has happened are either uninteresting or unconvincing as individuals. The significance has been neither in the action nor in the persons of the play. 'What we have written,' says Agatha, 'is not a story of detection, of crime and punishment, but of sin and expiation.' The problem is whether drama can deal with sin, and still be drama, or whether, like the law, it can only deal with crime.

Mr Eliot's three experiments in drama are closely related to the three stages in his poetic development. The two fragments which make up *Sweeney Agonistes*[1] attempt to handle dramatically his earlier themes. *Murder in the Cathedral* (1935) has much in common with *Ash Wednesday* and the Ariel poems; it has a Christian subject and it poses some of the same critical problems as *Ash Wednesday* in the contrast between its central theme of sanctity and the theme of the choruses. *The Family Reunion* (1939), unlike the others, anticipates rather than follows the poems it most resembles. Though it handles much of the experience of *Ash Wednesday*, it treats its religious theme without direct reference to Christian dogma or use of Christian symbolism. Coming between *Burnt Norton* and the remaining Quartets, it attempts to present dramatically the discovery which is their subject.

The two Sweeney fragments are called 'fragments from an Aristophanic melodrama': that is, a play interspersed with songs. What drama is apparent in them is simply the drama of contrast, or interruption. The opening conversation between the two girls, Dusty and Doris, about the absent Pereira, who 'pays the rent', is interrupted by the ringing of the telephone, and Dusty deals with the menace of Pereira with what she plainly feels is feminine *expertise*. The fortune-telling breaks off with the appearance of the two of spades—the 'Coffin'; but the thought of the coffin is pushed into the background by the arrival of the party and the fragment breaks off with vacuous social conversation and male boasting. In the second fragment the dramatic contrast is provided by the gloom of Sweeney, and his anecdote of the man who 'did a girl in' introduces melodrama of the other kind. The theme of *Sweeney Agonistes* is the boredom and horror that lie beneath the commonplace and the ugly.

[1] First printed in *The Criterion* (Oct. 1926 and Jan. 1927) and published in book form 1932.

This boredom and horror are masked by the 'telephones, gramophones, motor-cars, two-seaters, six-seaters, Citroën, Rolls-Royce', and all the paraphernalia of parties and drinks. They break out at the mention of Pereira, who cannot be put off for ever, and at the appearance of the two of spades—the 'Coffin'. They interrupt the party when Sweeney sardonically adapts the cannibal-isle joke to his own purpose, to make of it an image of life reduced to its three facts: 'Birth, and copulation, and death.' And in his story of the man who 'did a girl in' and

> kept her there in a bath
> With a gallon of lysol in a bath

horror appears as the neurotic response to boredom:

> Any man might do a girl in
> Any man has to, needs to, wants to
> Once in a lifetime, do a girl in.

This theme of the outer life of parties which tries to keep boredom at bay; and of the outer life of routine, taking in the milk and paying the rent, which accompanies the inner life of nightmare, certainly provides dramatic moments. But it is difficult to see how, if he ever intended to, Mr Eliot could have developed it into a play. For it is essentially a static theme. In his 'Dialogue of Dramatic Poetry' (1928) Mr Eliot makes one of his characters say: 'What great poetry is not dramatic? . . . Who is more dramatic than Homer or Dante? We are human beings, and in what are we more interested than in human action and human attitudes? Even when he assaults, and with supreme mastery, the divine mystery, does not Dante engage us in the question of the human attitude towards this mystery—which is dramatic?' We use the word 'dramatic' often rather loosely, usually to mean 'having some of the qualities of drama', notably surprise. But what qualities of drama can human attitudes by themselves have? Some attitudes are incipiently dramatic, but many are not even that. When Dante, at the close of the *Paradiso*, describes his attitude 'fixed, immovable, intent' and declares 'such at that light doth man become that to turn thence to any other sight could not by possibility be ever yielded', he is describing an attitude that is totally undramatic. In Heaven there can be no drama, for the life of drama is change. A situation is incipiently dramatic if it is on the point of change and we feel: 'This cannot go on; something *must* happen.' It is fully dramatic when we feel: 'Something *is* happening that is changing everything for those concerned.' And the drama has been completed when we reach a situation where we feel: 'Something *has* happened; everything is now different.' Attitudes can be thus incipiently dramatic or they can be the result of drama; and a change of attitude can give us drama, though if it is not expressed in action, or is not the cause of action, the drama will be of a rather rarified kind. The shock that arises from the contrast of two attitudes can give us something sufficiently like the surprise of drama for us to call Sweeney's monstrous story interrupting the party a dramatic moment. It is not drama, but it has some of the qualities of drama. But Sweeney himself in telling his story avoids its drama. What impresses him is the undramatic: the dead girl in the bath, the murderer wondering who is alive and who is dead, and the milkman's daily call. Sweeney's incapacity to express the horror at the heart of life in any terms he feels to be adequate, or that his hearers are likely to understand, suggests that the subject of the fragments is not even the contrast of inanity and despair, but the gulf fixed between those capable of awareness and those who are not: 'You don't see them, you don't —but *I* see them.' It is difficult to see how such a subject could be developed at all except by repetition; for it is impossible to imagine any change in the attitudes of Doris and Dusty and their guests. The theme of Mr Eliot's early verse finds supreme expression in *The Waste Land*, to which *Sweeney Agonistes* appears a rather sterile appendix. Confined within the limits of scenic presentation, with this limited circle of people, the 'boredom', which in *The Waste Land* seems universal, is capable of dismissal as an accident of a certain class and period; and the 'horror' is either trivial, and rather obviously symbolic, as in the telephone bell and the knocking, or grotesque as in Sweeney's anecdote from the *News of the World*.

But it seems likely that the impulse behind the fragments was less the impulse to write a play, than the wish to experiment in the writing of dramatic verse. Although *Sweeney Agonistes* looks back in its subject-matter, it looks forward in its style. The pageant-play *The Rock*, to an even greater degree, should not be thought of as a dramatic experiment, but as having provided Mr Eliot with an opportunity for writing another kind of dramatic verse: choric verse. The traditional distinction between the metres of dialogue and the metres of the choruses of a play is also a practical one. Choric speaking must be emphatic or the sense is lost: it must keep time, and cannot indulge in much variation of speed and tone. Many voices speaking together are incapable of the subtle modulations of a single voice, and of the innumerable variations from a regular metrical base that make up the music of poetry. If the metre is regular, choral speaking will soon reduce it to the monotony of sing-song. Anyone knows this who has had to listen to classes of children reciting in unison verse not written for this method of delivery. Choric verse must therefore be itself written in free metres; the necessary variety must be inherent in the metrical structure, in variation in the length of line, and the length of the breath units. Where dialogue approximates to speech, choric verse must approximate to chant.

The choruses of *The Rock*, which owe much to the rhythms of the Authorized Version, and to the Prayer-Book Psalms, have the simplicity of syntax, the emphatic repetitions, the rhythmical variety which choric verse must possess.

These experiments culminate in *Murder in the Cathedral*. The martyrdom of Becket was an obvious choice for a Canterbury play, made more attractive no doubt by the association of the saint's name. The theme of the conflict of the spiritual and the secular powers, the relation of Church and State, was topical, and is a subject on which Mr Eliot has spoken much in prose. The story of Becket's life would seem to hold great dramatic and tragic potentialities, for the 'deed of horror' takes place between persons who, though not closely related, as Aristotle thought best, were at least closely bound by old ties of friendship; and the deed has a peculiar horror by the addition of sacrilege to the guilt of murder. But although the conflict of Church and State is present in the play, it is subordinated to another theme, and the drama of personal relationships Mr Eliot deliberately avoids. The king does not appear and the knights are not persons, but at first a gang, and then a set of attitudes. They murder for an idea, or for various ideas, and are not shown as individuals, disturbed by personal passions and personal motives. The central theme of the play is martyrdom, and martyrdom in its strict, ancient sense. For the word martyr means witness, and the Church did not at first confine the word to those who sealed their witness with their blood; it was a later distinction that separated the martyrs from the confessors. We are not to think of a martyr as primarily one who suffers for a cause, or who gives up his life for truth, but as a witness to the awful reality of the supernatural. The actual deed by which Thomas is struck down is in a sense unimportant. It is not important as a dramatic climax towards which all that has happened leads. We are warned again and again that we are not watching a sequence of events that has the normal dramatic logic of motive, act, result, but an action which depends on the will of God and not on the wills of men:

> For a little time the hungry hawk
> Will only soar and hover, circling lower,
> Waiting excuse, pretence, opportunity.
> End will be simple, sudden, God-given.

Nothing prepares us for the consummation. We are told rightly that

> the substance of our first act
> Will be shadows, and the strife with shadows.

Thomas can hardly be said to be tempted, for the play opens so near its climax that any inner development is impossible. Except for the last, the temptations are hardly more than recapitulations of what has now ceased to tempt, an exposition of what has happened rather than a present trial; and the last temptation is so subtle and interior that no audience can judge whether it is truly overcome or not. 'Solus Deus cogitationes cordium cognoscere potest.' What spiritual pride lurks in a martyr's heart, even in his last agony, is not to be measured by the most subtle and scrupulous self-analyst, far less by any bystander. Though Thomas may say

> Now is my way clear, now is the meaning plain:
> Temptation shall not come in this kind again,

a question has been raised that cannot be answered dramatically and that has simply to be set aside. We have to take it for granted that Thomas dies with a pure will, or else, more properly, ignore the whole problem of motives as beyond our competence and accept the fact of his death. If in the first act the strife is with shadows, in the second there is no strife at all. The martyr's sermon warns us that 'a martyrdom is never the design of man', and that a Christian martyrdom is neither an accident nor 'the effect of a man's will to become a Saint'. The hero has only to wait for his murderers to appear:

> All my life they have been coming, these feet. All my life
> I have waited. Death will come only when I am worthy,
> And if I am worthy, there is no danger.
> I have therefore only to make perfect my will.

When the knights rush in the momentary drama of their irruption breaks against the calm of Thomas, and the murder takes place as a kind of ritual slaughter of an unresisting victim, a necessary act, not in itself exciting or significant.

The attempt to present in Thomas the martyr in will and deed, with mind and heart purified to be made the instrument of the divine purpose, is a bold one. Success is hardly to be expected. There is more than a trace in the Archbishop of the 'classic prig' who disconcerts us so deeply in Milton's presentation of the tempted Christ in *Paradise Regained*. There is a taint of professionalism about his sanctity; the note of complacency is always creeping into his self-conscious presentation of himself. He holds, of course, the pastoral commission, and it is right that he should teach his flock, but his dramatic function comes to seem less to be a martyr or witness, than to improve the occasion, to give an Addisonian demonstration of 'how a Christian can die'. Thomas is indeed less a man than an embodied attitude, for there is in this play an almost Gnostic contempt for personality and its expression in acts. When Thomas declares with some scorn

> You argue by results, as this world does,
> To settle if an act be good or bad.
> You defer to the fact,

he seems to have forgotten that the test of fruits is not only the world's test; it is deeply in the Gospels. When he announces 'I have only to make perfect my will', he speaks more as a Gnostic Sage than as a Christian Saint. Sanctity here appears too near to spiritual self-culture. The difficulty lies partly in the nature of dramatic presentation. The protagonist of any play must be conscious and aware; that is part of his function as protagonist. It is through him that the situation is made clear to us, and we recognize implications hidden from other persons in the drama. But if there is no true action, if the centre of the play is a state of mind, the protagonist can only be *self*-aware and *self*-conscious, and self-consciousness is incompatible with sanctity. Mr Eliot has conceived his hero as a superior person. The nature of his superiority can be expounded dramatically only by himself, for the play assumes a gulf between the saint and the ordinary man. Inevitably in the expounding the protagonist appears superior in the pejorative sense.

But for all its lack of action and its unconvincing protagonist, *Murder in the Cathedral* is intensely moving and at times exciting when performed. The real drama of the play is to be found in fact where its greatest poetry lies—in the choruses. The change which is the life of drama is there: from the terror of the supernatural expressed at the opening to the rapturous recognition of the 'glory displayed in all the creatures of the earth' in the last. The fluctuations of the chorus are the true measure of Thomas's spiritual conquest. They feel his failure of faith after the last temptation. They know obscurely that if sanctity is nothing in the end but a higher egoism, there is no value in any human goodness. Only if the heroic has meaning can the ordinary have dignity. They 'know and do not know'; for they feel the danger but mistake where safety lies:

> God is leaving us, God is leaving us, more pang, more pain, than birth or death.
> Sweet and cloying through the dark air

Falls the stifling sense of despair;
The forms take shape in the dark air:
Puss-purr of leopard, footfall of padding bear,
Palm-pat of nodding ape, square hyaena waiting
For laughter, laughter, laughter. The Lords of Hell are here.

If he is safe, they are safe too; if he is destroyed, they are destroyed. They implore him to save himself for their sake, but the safety he and they find is of another kind. They have to learn that there is no safety in flight, and no escape in obscurity from evil and death. They have to accept their share in the 'eternal burden, the perpetual glory': the burden of sin, the glory of redemption. In the great chorus before the martyrdom they identify themselves with a whole world groaning and travailing. The monstrous act they are about to witness is not an aberration, an eccentricity; it is an expression of the universal malice and corruption, which it is man's burden and glory to be conscious of. It is not something of which the common man is innocent. The evil plotted by potentates is the same evil as is met

in the kitchen, in the passage,
In the mews in the barn in the byre in the market place
In our veins our bowels our skulls.

They have to pierce deeper, beyond all agents and forms of evil, beyond death and judgment to

Emptiness, absence, separation from God.

In face of the intensity of the *Dies Irae* chorus, the ecstasy of penitence and shame that breaks out with the cry

Clear the air! clean the sky! wash the wind! take stone
from stone and wash them,

and the final chorus of praise, criticism of the presentation of the hero seems irrelevant; it is only a minor blemish. Although we may not get from *Murder in the Cathedral* the experience we normally look for in a play, the experience we do get cannot be called anything but dramatic. We identify ourselves with the women of the chorus; their experience communicates itself to us, and gives us the feeling we have been not spectators but sharers in a mystery.[1] We live through a *peripeteia*, we experience a great discovery. We pass with them through horror, out of boredom, into glory.[2]

Once again Mr Eliot has in fact gone back in order to go forward. He has returned to the most primitive form of tragedy. The model is the earlier plays of Aeschylus in which, as Professor Murray says, 'there is one great situation, in which the poet steeps our minds, with at most one or two sudden flashes of action passing over it. Woman pursued by the lust of unloved man, the Saviour of mankind nailed eternally to the rock, the suspense of a great people expecting and receiving the news of defeat in war, the agony of a besieged city—these are all the kind of subject that might be treated in a simple choral dance with nothing but words and music. At most Aeschylus, transforming the *Molpê* into drama, adds a brief flash of action: in the *Supplices* the rescue of the women, in the *Prometheus* the binding in the prologue and the casting into Hell at the end, in the *Seven* the scene where Eteocles goes out to kill his brother and to die. In the *Persae* there is a steady tension throughout, diversified by the entrance of the Messenger, the evocation of Darius, and the entry of Xerxes, but the situation is never changed, only seen from different angles.' When Professor Murray sums up Greek tragedy in a sentence, his words could be applied to *Murder in the Cathedral*:

[1] The power of the poetry triumphs over the curious costumes in which the 'poor women of Canterbury' are usually draped. They are made to look like young ladies who, for a charade, have done the best they could with a set of slightly old-fashioned artistic bedspreads.

[2] In an essay printed in *T. S. Eliot: A Symposium*, edited by Richard March and Tambimuttu, Mr Ashley Dukes says that 'the first draft of the Becket tragedy' was called 'Fear in the Way', and that the title *Murder in the Cathedral* was inspired by Mrs Martin Browne.

'Normally the play portrayed some traditional story which was treated as the *Aition* or origin of some existing religious practice.' Mr Eliot, invited to write a play for Canterbury, has begun where the earliest Greek dramatists would have begun, with the present fact: the veneration paid to the martyr by the Church for which he died. His play leads to its last words: 'Blessed Thomas pray for us.' The poor women of the chorus are prototypes of all those who, throughout the ages, will come to implore help from the hero-saint. They are the worshippers at the shrine, the pilgrims to Canterbury, the Christian equivalent of the ritual mourners weeping for the dead god or hero. But the play transcends its origin and occasion, and the chorus becomes humanity, confronted by the mystery of iniquity and the mystery of holiness.

Murder in the Cathedral is like *Ash Wednesday* in its choice of a Christian theme, its employment of liturgical material: the introits and versicles for the three days after Christmas, the *Dies Irae*, the *Te Deum*; and most of all in the contrast between the ideal of sanctity, which is at the centre, and the reality of the experience of common unsanctified humanity out of which both poem and play arise. But the symbolic figures of *Ash Wednesday*, by whom the idea of blessedness is communicated—the Lady of Silences and the veiled sister, existing in a world of dream and vision—are more satisfying to the imagination than Thomas, who has to endure the hard, clear light of the stage. Perhaps Mr Eliot tried too much with Thomas, and a more simple and conventional treatment of the central figure would have been less discordant with the truth and grandeur of the choruses.

The Family Reunion is a play of quite a different kind and the critical problem it presents is more acute. Unlike most poetic plays in modern times, it is more effective when acted than when read. It is full of dramatic clash and dramatic excitement. The drama is here at the centre. The hero experiences the change and makes the discovery; the chorus is static. The central figure is not a saint or a hero, but a man, who is shown at the very moment of turning, or conversion. The play attempts to present directly what *Ash Wednesday* took for granted: the discovery in experience of a meaning which re-integrates the whole personality, and changes the direction of the will. This experience is at the centre of the play; again where the greatest poetry is to be found, in the scenes between Harry and Mary, and Harry and Agatha, which are both highly dramatic and highly poetic. The story of the play is a modern story, which translates the myth of Orestes pursued by the Furies into terms of everyday life. What Greek influence there is in this play is to be looked for in the link between the plot and the Orestes myth, and seems to me to be quite superficial. Paradoxically Mr Eliot's Christian play, *Murder in the Cathedral*, is far more Greek in its spirit and form than this play, in which Christian terminology and explicitly Christian reference are deliberately avoided, and which at first sight demands comparison with the *Oresteia*, to which it so often refers.[1]

Although the symbol of the 'powers beyond us' is the Eumenides, they are employed in a way no Greek dramatist would have used them. They are purely symbols and have no dramatic life. They neither act nor speak, but simply appear, or do not appear. Apart from these mysterious shapes, the characters in the drama are persons living in the present century, associated with a certain class and with

[1] The comparison has been made very fully by Miss Maud Bodkin in *The Quest for Salvation in an Ancient and a Modern Play*, and I gladly acknowledge my debt to her exposition. I think the reason she gives for Mr Eliot's use of the Eumenides is the right one: 'It seems as though in writing a play so permeated by awareness of a spiritual world, yet with no direct reference to Christian forms of faith, Eliot had meant to avoid any unnecessary limiting of the communication of his thought.'

defined ways of life. They are not in any way mythical. Although we are constantly reminded of the House of Atreus, the characters remain within the bounds of realistic presentation. We never forget that we are in a house in Northern England, the house of a young man of property, whose aunt, Agatha, is the Principal of a college, and whose cousin, Mary, is thinking about taking up an academic career. The chorus is also entirely unlike any Greek chorus. It is a group of four quite distinct persons, who are at moments impelled to speak together to express their common bewilderment. Its members are conspicuous for their lack of comprehension. They are not interpreters to the audience of a story which without them might seem too remote from common experience. They seem present partly to warn us against certain misunderstandings by presenting them in an obviously absurd form, and partly as comic relief. Unlike the women of Canterbury, who carry the drama of *Murder in the Cathedral*, they do not change as the play proceeds. At the close, as at the beginning, their real anxiety is to 'do the right thing'. But the most important difference between *The Family Reunion* and any Greek drama is in the direct action. When Milton, at the close of *Samson Agonistes*, declared through his chorus:

> His servants he with new acquist
> Of true experience from this great event
> With peace and consolation hath dismist,
> And calm of mind all passion spent,

he was using words one could apply to any Greek play. In *The Family Reunion* there is no 'great event'. The direct action of the play can be briefly stated: it consists of the return of Harry, Lord Monchensey, to his home, after an absence of eight years, and his departure again, after about three hours, which causes the death of his mother from heart-failure. This is the 'event' with which the play deals;

it is not 'what happens', to use Harry's own distinction. We may use the Greek myth to help us in understanding 'what happens', but in form *The Family Reunion* is completely original, as original dramatically as *Four Quartets* is poetically.

The inner drama, the true play, is a play devised and controlled

> by powers beyond us
> Which now and then emerge.

In this play Harry, Agatha and Mary and, though she does not wish to and does not know it, Amy play their appointed parts. Harry's is the most important part, but Agatha has the clearest apprehension of the nature of the drama and knows from the beginning, not what is going to happen, but what kind of action they are involved in. She has to lead Harry, and give her direction to Mary, so that all three may play rightly the parts they have to play. Like an accomplished actress, prompting gifted amateurs, she 'carries the play', though not herself acting the chief role, and has her reward in the performance Harry gives. But there is a second play which has been designed by a human will. This is Amy's drama, which she has planned, and which she has invited all the characters to come and enact. In her play, the last eight years are to be ignored; the three sons are to be gathered together for their mother's birthday party, in order that Harry may take up his destined role as master of Wishwood, —Mary, it is hoped, will be able to fit in as Harry's wife, a scheme that had gone wrong once, but is now to be fulfilled. This drama of Amy's never really gets started. It collapses at the first appearance of Harry. But her will is set upon it, and she ignores his condition, as later she ignores the non-arrival of his brothers, and with the aid of Dr Warburton attempts by improvisation to get Harry to play his part. This drama she has planned and which she tries again and again to impose on the true drama she has finally to abandon when Harry announces his departure. Having always lived as the slave of the future, she finds the future taken from her; she is left at last alone with the present and 'the clock stops in the dark'. The chorus of aunts and uncles, snatched away from their harmless unnecessary occupations by Amy's imperious command, to act in her drama of Harry's home-coming, realize even before Harry's entry that things are not going as they should:

> Why do we feel embarrassed, impatient, fretful, ill at ease,
> Assembled like amateur actors who have not been assigned their parts?
> Like amateur actors in a dream when the curtain rises, to find themselves dressed for a different play, or having rehearsed the wrong parts,
> Waiting for the rustling in the stalls, the titter in the dress circle, the laughter and catcalls in the gallery?

The ironic comedy of the play arises because, though they realize that Amy's drama has gone wrong, they fail to penetrate into the true drama. They make ineffective efforts to turn 'what is happening' into the kind of play they might understand and in which they could play their parts with satisfaction, a play of 'detection, of crime and punishment'. At other times, when Amy's eye is on them they try to re-assume their old roles of the helpful aunts and uncles in-augurating the happy new régime. Although they vary in the extent of their stupidity or malice, Gerald being, as Amy says, the stupidest, Ivy the most snobbish, Violet the most malicious, and Charles the nicest, they agree in the end in a common statement of their inadequacy:

> We have lost our way in the dark.

These abortive efforts of the chorus to find out what it is all about and then to act properly are the main source of the comedy in *The Family Reunion*. There reappears here what had been missing from Mr Eliot's work since *Sweeney Agonistes*: the humour, irony and wit which were so delightful in his earlier poetry.[1] The humour of *The Family Reunion* has its root in the incongruities of family life: the irony of family conclaves over the younger generation; the malice that salts family conversation; and the personal dislike that can co-exist with a strong sense of the family bond. This is enriched by the poet's shrewd appreciation of the different social types the aunts and uncles represent, which, though it makes them unsuitable as choric characters, gives human variety to the drama. The escapade of Arthur provides comedy of another kind. The simple absurdity of his 'I thought it was all open country about here' is a welcome note of pure comedy, untinged with irony.

The interaction of the three dramas—the true drama of 'sin and expiation'; Amy's projected drama of a future not built upon the past; and the chorus's attempted drama of detection—is handled with remarkable skill. The exposition is particularly brilliant in its economy. We realize from the first moment the hostility between Amy and her younger sister Agatha. Agatha is the first of the assembled aunts and uncles to speak. She replies to Amy's 'Make up the fire. Will the spring never come? I am cold,' with what seems a mere commonplace: 'Wishwood was always a cold place, Amy.' Amy does not reply and Agatha remains silent during the consequent chatter, making no attempt to protect Mary from avuncular tactlessness. It is clear that two conflicting personalities are involved in this conventional exchange: the one a personality that demands and rebels, the other a personality that accepts and recognizes facts. We learn then that Mary, who is 'getting on for

---

[1] These gifts are fully exploited in *Old Possum's Book of Practical Cats*, though it is uncertain, in view of the poet's prefatory acknowledgment, how much is owing there to his youthful assistants, and even more to the fertile wit of the Man in White Spats.

thirty', had been designed by Lady Monchensey for her son's wife, and that she is unhappy and touchy about her spinsterhood. We have a strong impression of the dominating personality of Lady Monchensey, who has collected together against their will, for this family reunion, her three younger sisters and her late husband's two brothers. She declares:

> I keep Wishwood alive
> To keep the family alive, to keep them together,
> To keep me alive, and I live to keep them.

The clash between Amy and Agatha becomes more obvious when, in spite of Amy's dismissal of Mary's *gauche* exit: 'Meanwhile, let us drop the subject. The less said the better', Agatha insists on bringing 'the subject' up:

> It is going to be rather painful for Harry
> After eight years and all that has happened
> To come back to Wishwood.

The exposition is completed then by the conversation of the family. We learn that Harry made a disastrous marriage, with a person who, his mother says, 'never would have been one of the family'; that his wife was drowned at sea just about a year ago, and that the family are uncertain whether her death was accident or suicide, though Ivy's added: 'Swept off the deck in the middle of a storm' suggests accident. Lady Monchensey then lays down her plans, in a speech in which the word 'future' occurs three times within five lines. The family are to behave as if nothing has happened:

> Harry is to take command at Wishwood
> And I hope we can contrive his future happiness.

Agatha, in what is really a soliloquy, comments on this plan which neglects

> all the admonitions
> From the world around the corner,

and the four others express their uneasiness and embarrassment in unison, with an antiphonal expansion, in which each laments the harmless pleasures foregone at Amy's command.

The forebodings of the chorus are immediately justified by the entrance of Harry, whose condition makes nonsense of the drama of reunion for her birthday which Amy had planned. Ignoring the greetings of the assembled family he stares over their heads at the uncurtained window, declaring that here, at home, he at last sees the spectres whose eyes he had felt upon him throughout his haunted travels. With the question: 'Why here? Why here?', he breaks off to greet his mother and relations, and she, ignoring his state, attempts to re-assume direction of events by talk of business and the assurance that he will find nothing changed. The aunts and uncles take their cue from her and hastily pick up the roles she has cast them for, but Harry breaks in impatiently once more:

> You all of you try to talk as if nothing had happened,
> And yet you are talking of nothing else. Why not get to the point
> Or if you want to pretend that I am another person—
> A person that you have conspired to invent, please do so
> In my absence. I shall be less embarrassing to you.

But as he is about to leave the room he stops at Agatha, who checks him with the reminder that if he really wants no pretences he must make a beginning himself: he must try to make them understand. He answers with despair that he cannot explain; then, slowly, as if led on by Agatha, he begins the attempt to define his nightmare. What follows is profoundly ironic. As Harry searches for the phrases and images that will illuminate his darkness, encouraged in his self-exploration by Agatha, the real drama begins. He is listened to in silence by Amy, except for the one sharp cry: 'Harry!', by which she attempts to break the spell that is on him. But he provides his aunts and uncles at last with a clue, something definite if horrifying:

> It was only reversing the senseless direction
> For a momentary rest on the burning wheel
> That cloudless night in the mid-Atlantic
> When I pushed her over.

Here is an 'event', something that can be dealt with. They hastily adapt themselves and begin to deal in their different ways with the situation. But before they have time to get very far Amy intervenes. Unable to accept the failure of her plans, she sends Harry off to rest and to have a hot bath. It is the journey that has tired him; in the morning he will see that nothing has changed and will slip easily into the part prepared for him. The family then take up their new parts and concentrate on the problem of whether Harry has in reality killed his wife, or whether it is only a delusion. The first thing is to get a doctor, the second to do a little detective work on Harry's servant, Downing. The first suggestion Amy agrees to, but, significantly, only after she has asked Agatha's opinion, and with the assertion that she herself is the person to ring up the doctor. The cross-questioning of Downing takes place without her, and without Agatha, who knows it is pointless, though she agrees to it as she agreed to the summoning of the doctor as

> a necessary move
> In an unnecessary action.

The interview with Downing is dramatically important, not because of any assistance it gives his questioners in solving their problem of whether Harry is or is not a murderer, but because of what it tells the audience, incidentally, of his married life. Downing reveals the nervous, unstable, possessive temperament of the wife, and the nervous anxiety of the husband: the torment of two persons, one making endless claims which cannot be satisfied by the other, and the other feeling guilt and anxiety at his failure. After Downing's departure the aunts and uncles express their feeling of being out of their depth, and each in turn gives utterance to distrust of the others. They leave the stage to dress for dinner, shepherded by Amy, whose plans have received another set-back with the non-arrival of the two younger brothers. Their exit leaves the stage clear for the resumption of the true drama. Mary is given her part by Agatha after the brief conversation over the arranging of the flowers. She wants to escape, to leave Wishwood, to take up the academic career which Agatha had advised her to try for seven years ago. She asks about Harry's wife, the woman he chose instead of her. Now he has returned she sees that his mother's plan for him and for her is impossible. Both fear and pride make it intolerable for her to stay. But Agatha tells her she must wait:

> You and I, Mary,
> Are only watchers and waiters: not the easiest role:

and leaves her to face the thing she dreads, the interview with Harry. It begins with embarrassment; but at his need she forgets her ambiguous position, and speaks with candour of their early life together. The scene mounts to a great poetic climax, and then to a moment of intense drama when Harry recoils:

> Stop!
> What is that? do you feel it?

It ends with the spectres at the window, visible to Harry and to the audience, though not to Mary. Though Mary has fumbled at the beginning of her part, and has gone beyond it at the close when she cries:

> Look at me. You can depend on me.
> Harry! Harry! It's all *right*, I tell you.
> If you will depend on me, it will be all right,

she has fulfilled her role. She has made him see that the
Furies are here in his home and that he must face them here.
The dinner-party then assembles. The two younger brothers
have still not arrived but Amy decides to go on with her
party without them. The chorus follows her into dinner in
the grip of a 'most undignified terror' and Agatha completes the act with a prayer:

> There are three together
> May the three be separated
> May the knot that was tied
> Become unknotted
> May the crossed bones
> In the filled-up well
> Be at last straightened.

The second act takes place after dinner. It opens with
an interview between Dr Warburton and Harry in which
the two dramas cross. Warburton, who has been summoned
by Amy, is anxious to tell Harry of the state of his mother's
health, appealing to him to accede to her plans by arousing
his pity; but Harry sees him as someone who can explain to
him what lies behind the unhappiness of his childhood,
someone who can tell him about the missing figure in his
life, his father. The conversation is interrupted by the appearance of Sergeant Winchell. At first Harry is uncertain
whether the policeman is real or a figment of his haunted
imagination, and then he mistakes his errand:

> Why do you keep asking
> About her Ladyship? Do you know or don't you?
> I'm not afraid of you.

But Harry's lapse into the drama of 'crime and punishment'
is only momentary. He listens in silence to Winchell's
account of the accident that has prevented his brother
John's arrival, and for a moment he and his mother are
united in a common impatience at Ivy and Violet's inepti-

tude. He takes her gently from the room, returning when Warburton and Winchell have gone, to announce that she has fallen asleep. Plainly there has been no communication there. In a mood of irritation he speaks ironically to his aunts and uncles, mocking their concern with the unimportant, until he is recalled from this false note by Agatha, who once more shows him his proper part:

> To rest in our own suffering
> Is evasion of suffering. We must learn to suffer more.

He replies to her in quite another tone and is silent during the discussion of the next unimportant event: Arthur's accident and escapade. As the chorus go out to

> listen to the weather report
> And the international catastrophes,

he and Agatha, at last alone upon the stage, summon all their strength and courage to perform the parts they have to play. Their great scene ends with decision: Harry's 'I must go', echoed by Agatha's 'You must go', on which Amy enters. Her projected drama is now ruined beyond repair. She turns on Agatha as the cause of the disaster. The scene between the two sisters, after Harry has gone out, illuminates anything that was still dark. The naked truth is in Amy's terrible speech. She tells at last, because she recognizes at last, what the past was really like. The entrance of Mary, aghast at the news of Harry's departure, gives her a respite. She is silent while Agatha once more shows Mary her role. When she speaks again, still shaken by the horror of her scene with Agatha, she reveals her knowledge of the true present:

> An old woman alone in a damned house.

Her final explanation: 'Harry is going away—to become a missionary', may be a sop to the returned aunts and uncles, who settle on this tangible notion eagerly and make helpful, practical comments. Or perhaps it is a last attempt to preserve the facade of normality. It is impossible to say. At the end, however, she makes no pretence. It is too late for her to change in this life; she goes out to die. The reunion that was designed to take place

>in the day time
>And in the hither world,

had taken place

>in the night time
>And in the nether world
>Where the meshes we have woven
>Bind us to each other.

In the true drama of 'sin and expiation' a dead man and a dead woman: the unhappy father who died alone away from home, and the unhappy wife, drowned at sea, have been involved with the living Harry, Amy, Agatha and Mary. Harry's departure is for his own redemption and that of the departed, who may now rest in peace.

The discovery which Harry makes can be described in different ways. The simplest way to begin is to say that he learns from Agatha certain facts about his father, his mother and his aunt, which were kept from him through his childhood, but which, now he learns them, explain to him his wretchedness. He learns that his father's marriage, like his own, contained no ecstasy; that his mother, lonely and an alien in the house to which she had been brought as a bride, attempted to escape her loneliness by inviting her younger sister to live with her, and that his father and Agatha discovered one hot summer day in a flash of ecstasy and terror that they loved each other. He learns also that just before he was born his father was desperately turning over in his mind ways of destroying his unloved wife, and that Agatha stopped him. The marriage was preserved, and two more sons were born before the husband and wife parted by consent. But this story which Harry is told discovers to him his own story. When he hears of his father hiding 'his strength beneath unusual weakness, the diffidence of a solitary man'; and yielding to his mother's will, he understands the little boy for whom everything was arranged, whose only memory of freedom is 'a hollow tree in a wood by the river' where he played with Mary, and the husband whom Downing describes, as 'always very quiet' and 'very anxious about my Lady'. When he hears of those summer months when his father plotted to murder his mother, while Agatha thought of him as her child coming to birth, his obsession becomes 'true in a different sense' and slips from him:

> Perhaps my life has only been a dream
> Dreamt through me by the minds of others. Perhaps
> I only dreamt I pushed her.

As Agatha speaks to him of those months before his birth, she becomes the mother he had never found. The little boy, for whom everything was designed and planned, the man with a part to play that had been imposed on him, vanishes. When he cries 'And have me', and says:

> Look, I do not know why,
> I feel happy for a moment, as if I had come home,

family affection as a 'formal obligation, a duty only noticed by its neglect' has disappeared; in its place is the real relation he had never known. As Agatha speaks of that moment of ecstasy she had experienced as a girl, and of the long years of discipline and duty that followed, waiting for the moment when 'the chain breaks', and he tells of his own existence among shadows, till the moment when he found himself alone, his excitement mounts. It is not only a mother he finds. In a flash he becomes his father, on that summer day years ago, looking up to see Agatha enter through the little door of the rose-garden. Just as for a moment he has been the child he might have been, he becomes for a moment the lover he never was, freely encountering love with love.

Up to this moment it is possible to speak in purely psychological terms: to see Agatha as a kind of analyst who helps Harry to discover in his relation to his parents the reasons for the failure of his marriage, and to rid himself therefore of his obsessive feeling of guilt. But at this moment, once again, the figures of the Eumenides appear, visible to Agatha as they had not been to Mary, and visible again to the audience. Their reality is finally confirmed by Downing's speech at the end of the play. Downing who is not a member of the family, not involved in this drama of hatreds and despairs, is perfectly aware of their presence, though he knows they have nothing to do with him. Their presence makes necessary another set of terms than the psychological. The Eumenides become visible only twice. At their first appearance they recall Harry at the climax of his interview with Mary, from the vision she offers him of 'Singing and light'. When they first appear, it is to call him back to recognition of his sin. He tries to deny it:

> When I knew her, I was not the same person.
> I was not any person. Nothing that I did
> Has to do with me.

Yet he knows in his heart that what Mary offers him is something he cannot take. She offers him again what he had already found wanting. She does not really understand. At their second appearance, after his release through Agatha, he greets their re-appearance quietly:

> and this time
> You cannot think that I am surprised to see you.
> And you shall not think that I am afraid to see you.
> This time, you are real, this time, you are outside me,
> And just endurable. I know that you are ready,
> Ready to leave Wishwood, and I am going with you.

He knows now what the sin really is, and so he knows why they have come. They are no longer Furies. When he next speaks of them they are 'the bright angels': messengers. Once he can acknowledge the awful truth: 'Behold I was shapen in wickedness and in sin hath my mother conceived me': he can see what is demanded of him and what is promised: 'But lo, thou requirest truth in the inward parts and shalt make me to understand wisdom secretly.' Although Agatha explains she does not explain away. The Eumenides are not projections of Harry's sense of guilt, any more than the sin he has to expiate is an unreal sin. The sin remains: it is his birth sin, the 'sin where he begun, which is his sin, though it was done before'. Conceived and brought forth in hatred not in love, he bears the sins of his parents, at once their victim and their perpetuator, for he has been himself incapable of love. Mary's 'ordinary hopelessness', and his wife's wretchedness are fruits of this sin, his parents' and his own, the sin of failure in loving. He has to learn to love. He must go away into solitude and silence, like the scapegoat, laden with sin, driven out into the wilderness, so that years later, or months—we do not know how long it may be—he may find what ways of love are possible for him. What is impossible is that he should remain at Wishwood, where his mother does not want what he can give, and where Mary, who does not share his burden of knowledge, can be hurt by his presence and the gulf between them. He is sustained by the discovery that he is loved. There are not eyes spying and watching to find him out; there is a 'single eye above the desert'. He is led by

> love and terror
> Of what waits and wants me, and will not let me fall.

At this climax of the play the critical problem arises. Up to the moment when Harry sees the spectres for the second time and recognizes why they have come, the dramatic excitement and the psychological truth of the play carry us forward. But they carry us to a frontier which drama cannot cross. The climax is a dramatic anti-climax. The play ends with Harry's departure and his mother's death. Agatha presumably returns to her college and Mary goes away to take up some kind of career. The single one of these events that can be called dramatic is Amy's death, and the dramatist has to seize on that to round off his play. The true meaning of the play is not, however, in Amy's death, which is merely a consequence, but in Harry's conversion; and that, like Thomas's sanctity, we have to take for granted. It cannot be expressed in dramatic terms. No answer is given or can be given to Amy's question: 'Why are you going?' or to the other question: 'Where are you going?' The audience is no wiser than the chorus. We can use psychological terms and say that Harry's departure is an act by which he expresses the end of his mother-fixation, or we can use religious terms and say that Harry's departure expresses his discovery that his obligation is not to his mother, but to God; that he is one of those who are called to 'leave all and follow'. Neither conception gives us a true ending to a play. On the one hand we are left asking for what purpose Harry has thus purged his imagination and broken his chains; what he is going to do with his freedom. On the other we are left, if we accept the dramatist's interpretation of life, with the question that must often have occurred to Ananias during the years in which Paul 'conferred not with flesh and blood'. As he remembered the street which is called Straight and the blind man, whom he had found there praying, whose sight he had restored and whom he had baptized as a 'chosen vessel of the Lord', he must have wondered, as time went on and he heard nothing of his convert, whether the chosen vessel was only one of the many called but not chosen. It is sometimes said carelessly that *The Family*

Reunion is about someone who becomes a saint. But, as the dramatist does not use the word, it is better perhaps not even to say that it is about someone called to be a saint, except in the sense that all Christians are so called. The particular calling Harry receives, his 'election' to use his own word, is to do for a purpose what many have to do without knowing why: endure loneliness, separation and suffering. He is one of those elected, in St Paul's mysterious words, to 'fill up that which is behind of the afflictions of Christ'. At the heart of the play is the Christian doctrine of the Atonement, and the mysterious exchanges of sin and suffering in the spiritual world through which mankind partakes in that mystery. This call Harry perceives and he leaves to follow it. Whether he will fulfil his calling, or how, we do not know. His exit is not an end but a beginning.

The failure to render the climax of the drama in dramatic terms is paralleled by a certain unreality in the *dramatis personae*. At the centre there is someone without a face; or at least he has many faces, Mr Eliot's own, or ours. It is extremely difficult to believe in Harry as a person, to accept with any conviction his station in life, to imagine him at any time when he is not revealing his distress. As for Agatha, she is quite incredible as the 'efficient principal of a women's college', and it is difficult to believe in the efficiency if she really had to spend as much of her energy as she suggests in 'trying not to dislike women'. I cannot imagine any body of Fellows in the world consenting to her election as Principal. Mary's intellectual ambitions and her intellectual interests are equally unplausible. These featureless persons are surrounded by a chorus of persons whose features are too fixed: in a set of unchanging comic masks. The characters at the centre are presented almost wholly from within; the surrounding characters almost wholly from without. The only character who approaches full dramatic realization is Amy. She is capable of surprising us, and her terrible quarrel with Agatha endows Agatha with something of her own reality. For all my admiration for *The Family Reunion*, and in spite of the power it has to move me on the stage even more than in the reading, though in it Mr Eliot has succeeded in his wish to 'convey the pleasures of poetry' to audiences of theatre-goers, the subject seems to me to be incapable of dramatic treatment. Both plot and persons fail to reveal to us, as drama must, a spectacle for our contemplation. Because there is no real action there are no real persons.

It is in *Four Quartets* that the subject of *The Family Reunion* finds completely satisfying artistic expression. In the third movement of each separate poem the moment of turning is expressed in the poetry and leads to a poetic solution in the fifth, which in each poem provides a true poetic climax. But the progress from *Burnt Norton* to *Little Gidding* would hardly have been possible without *The Family Reunion*. The bold flexibility of the verse in the later Quartets, its confidence and daring and ease, were made possible by the achievement of *The Family Reunion* with its control over transitions, its changes of rhythm, its power of 'expressing the greatest thoughts naturally'. On the other hand, the growth in the subject throughout *Four Quartets* up to *Little Gidding*, with its emphasis upon the historical, makes us hope that Mr Eliot may yet write a great drama, in which 'what happens' is expressed in a great event.

CHAPTER VII

THE APPROACH TO THE MEANING

And approach to the meaning restores the experience
In a different form, beyond any meaning
We can assign to happiness.

The Dry Salvages

'After sharpe shoures', quod Pees   'moste shene is the sonne;
Is no weder warmer   than after watery cloudes.
Ne no loue leuere   ne leuer frendes,
Than after werre and wo   whan Loue and Pees be maistres.
Was neuere werre in this worlde   ne wykkednesse so kene,
That ne Loue, and hym luste   to laughynge ne broughte,
And Pees thorw pacience   alle perilles stopped . . .
For impossible is no thyng   to hym that is almyghty.'

Piers Plowman, B xviii

But that his care conserveth
As Time, so all Time's honours too,
Regarding still what heaven should do
And not what earth deserveth.

BEN JONSON:
The Golden Age Restored

THE discovery, symbolized by the waking from sleep of the old king Pericles in *Marina*, which the chorus makes in *Murder in the Cathedral*, and which Harry makes in *The Family Reunion*, is given to us without the use of myth or narrative in *Four Quartets*, by means of various images, and by changes in the rhythms of the poetry. This discovery, which is at the heart of each of the four poems, can be described in different terms in each poem, but essentially all four poems are one poem, and the central discovery of each is the same discovery. The growth of the subject throughout the poem is a growth in the apprehension of its significance. As the significance is appreciated more fully, the experience itself becomes more tangible, and the world in which it takes place gains in richness and reality.

Each of the four poems takes its title from a place, and the experience of each is expressed in imagery which arises from a deeply felt sense of place and time. In *Burnt Norton*, as has been said, the place has no particular associations. The time has no particular significance either; it is any summer afternoon. East Coker is a Somersetshire village, from which in the seventeenth century Andrew Eliot set out for the New World. The poet is staying there in the late summer, and his mind is full of the thought of his family and ancestors. The Dry Salvages are a group of rocky islands off the coast of Massachusetts, part of the landscape of the poet's childhood, and part of the new experience of his ancestors after they had crossed the seas. This poem is not about a place visited, but a place once lived in, remembered with the peculiar vividness with which we remember the landscape of our childhood. Little Gidding, on the other hand, has historic not personal associations. It is a village in Huntingdonshire to which Nicholas Ferrar and his family retired in order to lead a common life of devotion. It is visited by the poet on a winter's afternoon. He goes there to pray in the chapel.

Burnt Norton is a land-locked poem; its whole feeling is enclosed. It builds up by suggestion rather than statement a picture of a house and formal garden, and of a way of life which is social and civilized. The picture gradually given is of shrubbery and alley-walk, rose-garden, box-edgings, and a pool. There are sunflowers in the borders and clematis hanging from the wall and clipped yews. The references to dust on a bowl of rose-leaves, to a Chinese jar, and to the music of the violin give the same impression of a way of life that is cultured and refined. The image used at the climax of the children laughing among the leaves of the garden is an image of human happiness, of 'la douceur de la vie'. It has been suggested to me that the setting of the poem and the image of the laughing hidden children may have been caught from Rudyard Kipling's story *They*. The children in that story are both 'what might have been and what has been', appearing to those who have lost their children in the house of a blind woman who has never borne a child.

The poem opens with a meditation on the relation of past, present and future, and on the persistence in memory of what might have been as well as of what has been. The first image that occurs is of footfalls that

> echo in the memory
> Down the passage which we did not take
> Towards the door we never opened
> Into the rose-garden.

What the purpose of such memories is the poet cannot say; they disturb the 'dust on a bowl of rose-leaves', stirring something dead and buried in the present. The garden also is full of echoes, and in the garden what might have been and what has been, for a moment, are. In stillness, silence and light, what never was, and what was, is, for a space, real; the dream of innocent human happiness is felt again as truth. Then the moment passes. The bird's call, which had been an invitation, becomes a warning: 'Go, go, go, said the bird.'

The second movement opens with a passage of great poetic beauty, in which the unity of experience is conveyed by the juxtaposition of contraries. This passage is not susceptible of too close analysis. Its opening line: 'Garlic and sapphires in the mud', inspired by Mallarmé's jewel imagery,[1] is an image of the variety contained in a single sense impression: the soft and the hard, vegetable and

---

[1] Mr Eliot seems to have had in mind two phrases of Mallarmé: 'Tonnerre et rubis aux moyeux' from the poem 'M'introduire dans ton histoire', and 'bavant boue et rubis' from the sonnet 'Le Tombeau de Charles Baudelaire'.

mineral, the living and growing and the petrified and glittering, the common and the precious, the scented and the scentless. The 'trilling wire in the blood', the nervous tingling in our veins, runs on below old wounds, healed and not healed, and the movement within our bodies, which are ever in flux, is akin to the movement we perceive among the stars, drifting in the milky way like the atoms of Democritus, and to the flow of summer sap in the trees. We are at the same time aware of the dance of light upon the leaves from above, and of the pursuit of boar by boarhound below, and of this same pursuit and flight among the stars. At once all is flux, yet all is pattern; and from the thought of pattern the poet turns to think of how we apprehend pattern: from a point. This 'still point' is the theme of the second half of the movement, where the relation of stillness and movement, of the moment that is not in time and of living in time, is considered. We come back at the close to memory with which the meditation began.[1]

In the third movement there is an abrupt change. We have left the garden and the images of nature for a world which is in every way different. The first paragraph reminds us of *The Waste Land*'s vision of the crowd flowing over London Bridge, the slaves of time, each one imprisoned in his own solitude. Here we are in the twilight world of the London Tube. This image of passengers is central to *Four Quartets*; it occurs at this point in each of the first three poems. At this first use of the image we are shown travellers borne along in what is neither daylight nor darkness, their 'time-ridden faces' 'filled with fancies and empty of meaning'. Passing from one station to another, they find no meaning in the present, it is only a stop between where

[1] I believe the passage beginning 'At the still point of the turning world' owes something to the description of the magical dance of the Tarot figures in *The Greater Trumps* by Charles Williams.

they have come from and where they are going to.[1] The
second paragraph calls for a halt. To the boredom of the
underground journey it opposes a deliberate acceptance of
what lies behind the boredom. The mind instead of ignoring
its solitude and misery, instead of disregarding the desert, is
asked to accept it: to recognize its destitution and to enter
the present. It must leave the movement of the world through
past, present and future, the journey from nowhere, through
nowhere, to nowhere, and realize its actual situation. This
method of entering the present is what is called the negative
way. Christianity has always found room in itself for both
types of spiritual experience: that which finds all nature a
theophany, and that which feels the truth of Pascal's
favourite text: 'Vere Tu es Deus absconditus.' This
deliberate descent into darkness out of twilight is 'one way'.
It is the same, the poet tells us, as the other: the undeliberate
ascent into the world of light which we read of in the first
movement. There we were told of an unsought experience,
of a moment in which the mind suddenly felt at home,
accepted, free from anxiety, 'the practical desire'. A moment
such as this cannot be held, though it can be remembered.
It happens unexpectedly as a grace, without the mind's pre-
paring itself or making any effort. The laughter of the children was a lovely surprise. Both experiences, the experience
of desolation and the experience of joy, release us from
slavery to 'time past and time future'. Each is a moment of
freedom.

The lovely lyric movement brings us back to the garden.
It is purely natural in its imagery. It is a lyric of twilight;
but this is a twilight of another kind; it is full of expectancy.
The light has gone, the cloud has shadowed the sun. We

[1] Compare *The Rock*:

> The desert is not remote in southern tropics,
> The desert is not only around the corner,
> The desert is squeezed in the tube-train next to you.

are living in time; but we wait in time for a touch: the touch of life or of death, a touch of tenderness or a touch of foreboding.

The last movement recurs to the ideas of the first. It begins once more with the thought of time and movement as necessary for pattern, and finds its images in the world of art, distinguishing between the stillness of a single note and the stillness of the whole work which includes its movement. But as the rhythm changes at the close the images of the first movement recur: the sunlight breaks out again, the dust is once more disturbed, innocent joy floods the heart, and the process of time seems unreal and ridiculous, 'stretching before and after' the moments of illumination.

The subject of *Burnt Norton* can be defined in various ways. If we adopt the method of commentators on *The Divine Comedy*, we may distinguish a literal, a moral and a mystical meaning. The literal meaning is simply that the poet has felt a moment of inexplicable joy, a moment of release, like the moment Agatha speaks of when she looked 'through the little door, when the sun was shining on the rosegarden'. It is a moment of escape from the endless walking 'down a concrete corridor', or 'through the stone passages of an immense and empty hospital'. This moment of release from the deadening feeling of meaningless sequence, 'in and out, in an endless drift', 'to and fro, dragging my feet', into the present, the moment when, in Agatha's phrase, 'the chain breaks', is connected here with the memory of 'what might have been'. The poem springs from this experience, and it sets by it another experience, which is sought deliberately, but which is the same, for 'the way up is the way down'. If we pass from the literal to the moral meaning we may say that the virtue to which *Burnt Norton* points us is the virtue of humility: a submission to the truth of ex-

perience, an acceptance of what is, that involves the acceptance of ignorance:

> Internal darkness, deprivation
> And destitution of all property,
> Desiccation of the world of sense,
> Evacuation of the world of fancy,
> Inoperancy of the world of spirit.

If we pass then to the use of theological terms we may say
that mystically the subject of *Burnt Norton* is grace: the
gift by which we seek to discover what we have already been
shown.

East Coker is much less confined in its setting; its background is a village and its environs, a landscape full of
human history, but history of a ruder, less cultivated kind.
It is set in a countryside where the sea is not far off, and the
sea-wind can be felt. The first movement ends with a lightly
touched reference to the sea; the sea provides an image of
overwhelming desolation at the close of the second; and
the final impulse of release and adventure is given by the
image of 'the vast waters of the petrel and the porpoise'.
The village is seen in its setting of open fields, and the
manor house is felt as part of the village. There is talk of the
rhythm of the seasons and the rhythm of the work of the
farm. The metaphors used for reality are mostly non-
human: the winter lightning, the wild strawberry, the
whisper of running streams; the images of desolation are
the dark wood, the brambles and rocks.

East Coker is not, like *Burnt Norton*, about a particular
experience. It is a meditation on the passage of time, felt
in the lifetime of an individual, who is now 'in the middle
way', and in the life of mankind generally. It opens with an
inversion of the motto on Mary Stuart's chair of state: 'In
my end is my beginning.' Inverted to 'In my beginning is
my end', this appears as a statement of rigid determinism,

and the first paragraph of the poem establishes by powerful rhythms and repetitions the cyclic view of human life and human history. The life of man and of mankind, and of the works of man is shown to have the same pattern as that of all life on the earth: an endlessly recurring succession of birth, growth, decay and death. This statement is repeated in the third paragraph, where the dead villagers are seen dancing round the bonfire, in death as in life 'keeping the rhythm'.[1] Contrasted, within the first movement, with the two statements of life as rhythm, pattern, sequence, are two passages in which the idea of stillness and rest is given. There is first the picture of the village sleeping in the hot silence of a late summer afternoon, and, at the close, the delicate hint of the breathless stillness of the dawn of a hot day. The notion of pattern and repetition leads only to despair: 'Feet rising and falling.' (This was Agatha's image for the sensation of imprisonment in time.) 'Eating and drinking. Dung and death.'

The lyrical passage with which the second movement opens contradicts both the rigid order and the stillness of the first. The idea of pattern is rejected, but so is the idea of peace. The seasons are all disordered. Spring thunder peals in November; the flowers of high summer jostle those of spring and winter. There is war too among the constellations, ending with the apocalyptic vision of the end of the

[1] The dancing figures round the bonfire are described in words taken from Sir Thomas Elyot's *The Governour*, where he praises dancing as a type of matrimony. The archaic spelling calls attention to the quotation, which, though apt in a poem dealing with the poet's ancestors, seems to me a little precious.

In an article in *Life and Letters* 1945, Professor Haussermann quotes Mr Eliot as having written to him: 'I think that the imagery of the first section (though taken from the village itself) may have been influenced by recollections of *Germelshausen*, which I have not read for many years.' Professor Haussermann adds that *Germelshausen* is a story 'in which a whole parish is punished by the Pope's interdict. It can neither live nor die. Once every hundred years it resumes for the space of one day its ghostly revelry, and then sinks again under the earth'.

world, burnt out to an icy cinder. But this romantic vision of chaos the poet rejects, for a plain, almost prosaic, statement of the same chaos in the life of the individual. There too we find no ordered sequence, pattern or development. The metaphor of autumnal serenity is false applied to man; experience does not bring wisdom, nor old age peace. The time when one knows never arrives, and the pattern is falsified by every new moment. We are always in the dark wood, in which Dante found himself in the middle of his life, the wood 'where the straight way is lost'. As we try to hold the past it slips from us, engulfed in the darkness of the present:

> The houses are all gone under the sea.
>
> The dancers are all gone under the hill.

The third movement takes up the theme of the third movement of *Burnt Norton*, though it has come to the darkness by a different road. It opens with blind Samson's cry of anguish, but this anguish soon turns to a sombre triumph. The darkness, in which we are lost, swallows up and hides from us the base, the trivial and the ignoble, the meaningless pomps and vanities of the world. The poet rejoices in this victory of the dark, in the same way as the writers of the early seventeenth century rejoiced in the levelling power of death. Once again we are reminded of the earlier verse, as we read the catalogue of illustrious nobodies:

> The captains, merchant bankers, eminent men of letters,
> The generous patrons of art, the statesmen and the rulers,
> Distinguished civil servants, chairmen of many committees,
> Industrial lords and petty contractors.

But this welcome to the darkness takes another turn: it is welcomed not only because it obliterates, but because it reveals. Within the darkness is light; within the stillness, movement and dancing; within the silence, sound. The image of passengers is subtly different in its use here. The darkness 'comes upon' the mind; it is not sought, but accepted. The watcher in the theatre, waiting in darkness while the scene changes, the passenger in the tube, when the train 'stops too long between stations', the patient half-etherized are all passive images. The activity required is simply waiting.

The tradition Mr Eliot is here writing in is a tradition that goes back beyond Christianity to the Neo-Platonists, who turned what had been a method of knowing—the dialectical method of arriving at truth by successive negations of the false—into a method of arriving at experience of the One. This doctrine of ascent or descent into union with reality, by successively discarding ideas which would limit the one idea of Being, found a natural metaphor in darkness and night. It was a double-edged metaphor, since night expressed both the obliteration of self and all created things, and also the uncharacterized Reality which was the object of contemplation. The anonymous English mystic who wrote in this tradition in the fourteenth century used for his symbol a cloud, and called his book *The Cloud of Unknowing*. He taught that the soul in this life must be always between two clouds, a cloud of forgetting beneath, which hides all creatures and works, and a cloud of unknowing above, upon which it must 'smite with a sharp dart of longing love'. 'For of all other creatures and their works, yea, and of the works of God's self, may a man through grace have fullhead of knowing, and well can he think of them: but of God Himself can no man think. And therefore I would leave all that thing that I can think, and choose to my love that thing that I cannot think. For why; He may well be loved, but not thought. By love may He be gotten and holden; but by thought never.' The actual phrase 'a cloud of unknowing' occurs in *The Family Reunion*, and a line in *Little Gidding* comes directly from the book; but in *East Coker* the great paradoxes of the negative way are taken from its most famous doctor, St John of the Cross. The riddling passage at the close of the first movement is an almost literal rendering of the maxims under the 'figure' which stands as frontispiece to *The Ascent of Mount Carmel*, and which appear in a slightly different form at the close of the thirteenth chapter of the first book of that treatise.[1] This deliberately unpoetical close leads us towards the fourth movement, which breaks upon the ear with majestic firmness, and shocks the mind by its powerful imagery.

The lyrical movement also unites despair and triumph, but now in the contemplation of human pain. If to know you must know nothing, then to live you must die. *East Coker* is far more concerned with the response made to experience than *Burnt Norton* is; and the experience to which response has to be made is the experience of a lifetime: the tragic experience of loss, deprivation, homelessness. The lyric is a poem on the Passion, thought of not as a single historic event, but as an eternal act perpetually operative in time, and the Passion is linked with the Eucharist. The

---

[1]   In order to arrive at having pleasure in everything,
     Desire to have pleasure in nothing.
         In order to arrive at possessing everything,
     Desire to possess nothing.
         In order to arrive being everything,
     Desire to be nothing.
         In order to arrive at knowing everything,
     Desire to know nothing.
         In order to arrive at that wherein thou hast no pleasure,
     Thou must go by a way wherein thou hast no pleasure.
         In order to arrive at that which thou knowest not,
     Thou must go by a way that thou knowest not.
         In order to arrive at that which thou possessest not,
     Thou must go by a way that thou possessest not.
         In order to arrive at that which thou art not,
     Thou must go through that which thou art not.
     (*The Complete Works of St John of the Cross*, translated by E. Allison Peers, vol I, p. 62).

grave heavy beat of the lines, the rigid stanza form, the mood, the paradoxes, the sense of tragic triumph which the rhythm holds, make this lyric like an early Passion hymn:

> Salve ara, salve victima,
> de passionis gloria,
> qua vita mortem pertulit
> et morte vitam reddidit.

In the final movement the feeling that every moment is a new moment, and every end a beginning—that the past is alive in the present, modifying it and itself being modified by it—is at first applied to the poet and his problem of expression. The mood seems not far from despair, except for the emphasis on effort. But as the rhythm alters the mood alters; effort becomes something nearer to adventure. The conception is applied to the life of individuals, with its complicated pattern in which both dead and living are involved, and a new image is introduced. In place of the travellers borne along on 'metalled ways', there are explorers. This is an image of free movement, for the explorer is free to range as he wishes, to lose and find his way, and to return to where he started from to begin his search again. The poem ends with the injunction to be 'still and still moving'; that we may pass 'through the dark cold and the empty desolation' to the open waters of the sea, which men have always regarded as a symbol of eternity. The close is typical of the whole poem, at once terrifying and exalting; it bids us 'launch out into the deep'.

The subject of *East Coker* in the literal sense is age: the recognition that life is more than half over, that time has passed and will pass yet more swiftly, and that in common with all mankind we have to die. It is a poem of earth: 'Dust we are to dust returning.' In the moral sense the subject is faith. It accepts the necessity of the humility of *Burnt Norton*:

The only wisdom we can hope to acquire
Is the wisdom of humility: humility is endless.

But it adds to the acceptance of ignorance in *Burnt Norton* an act of faith. It declares that the darkness is the darkness of God, and waits upon him. In the mystical sense the subject is the Atonement: the dogma that in darkness and death man is not alone, and that through them God and man are mysteriously reconciled.

The Dry Salvages has for its landscape the sea-coast of New England; its dominant imagery is of rocks and the sea. This landscape of his childhood Mr Eliot used in the final section of *Ash Wednesday*, looking on it there with longing as on a world hard to renounce. As always when he writes of the sea the poetry has great freedom and power; and in this poem, for the first time in the Quartets, the natural imagery is used boldly and beautifully, and, as it were, for its own sake. The landscape of *The Dry Salvages* is a landscape remembered, for this poem is not about the present, but about the past as it is known in the present, in our consciousness of it through memory.

The first movement is built on the contrast between two metaphors: the river of life and the sea of life. The river is an old metaphor for the life of man, and its flow here is linked with the flow of the seasons from spring to winter, and that of man's life from birth to death. The river is a reminder of what we should like to forget: our bondage to nature. Though it can for a time be ignored, it can assert its power by catastrophe as well as by its inevitable progress. 'The river is within us.' We feel it in our pulses. This is our earliest conception of time; something we become aware of by the change of seasons, and by our own growth. The images of the brown Mississippi, and of the ailanthus tree, a Southern tree, come naturally to the poet from his childhood in St Louis. The sea is time of another kind, the time of history and the time beyond history; the 'vast seas of time'. Individual man launches himself on this ocean of life and makes his short voyage, one of innumerable similar voyages. 'The sea is all about us.' This is a later conception of time, a conception we arrive at not through the senses, but through the imagination. The images here of the New England coast, with the fir-tree, characteristic of the landscape of the North, and the foreign fishermen, the Portuguese sailors found in colonies along that coast, belong to a later stage in the poet's life. This metaphor of the tossing seas of time denies the cyclic view of history: the biological interpretation, which imposes on events the rhythm of a succession of rivers, each culture being first young and vigorous, then mature, and finally decayed and outworn. It also denies the doctrine of progress which finds in history an upward development. We have instead a meaningless perpetual flux, a repetition without a pattern, to which each separate voyage adds nothing but itself. Yet through the apparently incoherent restlessness of the sea, there is carried to our ears the rhythm of the ground swell, different from the rhythm of the river, which we hear in our heart-beats, coming from the very depth of the ocean itself:

> And the ground swell, that is and was from the beginning,
> Clangs
> The bell.

The reminiscence of the doxology gives us the implication of the symbol of the ground swell, which makes itself felt in our hearts by the bell. The bell sounds a warning and a summons: it demands a response. Like the Angelus it is a call to prayer, and a commemoration of the mystery of the Incarnation; like the bell at the consecration it is a call to worship, and announces the presence of Christ; like the tolling bell it reminds us of our death, and calls us to die daily.[1]

The sestina with which the second movement opens is a poem on these several annunciations. Under the metaphor of fishermen setting out on their perilous voyages, over an ocean 'littered with wastage', it pictures the lives of individual men, the sum of which makes history. It finds meaning only in the union of the temporal with the eternal, in annunciations: the calamitous annunciation of terror and danger, the last annunciation of death, and the one Annunciation of history. The only *end* to the flux of history is man's response to the eternal manifesting itself in time. As in *The Waste Land*, it is by 'the awful daring of a moment's surrender' that we exist, by praying

> the hardly, barely prayable
> Prayer of the one Annunciation.

The meaningless monotony and pointless waste of living finds its purpose in the Virgin's words: 'Be it unto me according to thy word.'

As in the other poems the idea of the lyrical passage, given in metaphor and symbol, is then translated into the experience and idioms of every day. The past does not die;

[1] The best comment I can make on this symbol of the bell is to quote a passage from François Mauriac's *Dieu et Mammon*, where he speaks of the Annunciation of history and the annunciations of our individual lives, and links the summons of God with the sense of freedom in the soul. 'Aussi souverainement que son Incarnation a partagé l'histoire humaine, Jésus-Christ cherche la seconde propice pour s'insérer dans ce destin, pour s'unir à ce flot de chaque destinée particulière, pour introduire sa volonté dans cette apparente fatalité, pour détruire enfin cette fatalité. Tentatives quelquefois cachées et comme détournées, renouvelées à longs intervalles, souvent directes, impérieuses, pressantes comme une occasion unique et solennelle, mais qui donnent toujours à l'homme le plus asservi le sentiment qu'il demeure maître du oui ou du non. Il a pu croire, à l'approche de la tentation trop connue, qu'aucune force au monde ne l'empêcherait d'y succomber, et que ce péché familier était vraiment l'acte qu'il ne dépendait pas de lui de ne pas commettre. Mais voici que devant l'insistance de cette force qui demande à absorber sa faiblesse, tout d'un coup, il se voit terriblement libre.'

the annunciations, whether of happiness—'the sudden illumination'—or of agony, are permanent 'with such permanence as time has'. They are a part of our experience, recurring, preserved in memory by time. The pattern of the past is not a mere sequence, neither is it a development: if it were we could disown it and look to the future. But we cannot disown our past, which includes the past of others, and the past of the human race; it lives within us, never outgrown, revived as a reality as we understand its meaning.

The third movement turns to the future, which can only be built 'upon the real past'. Mr Eliot introduces here, as he had in *The Waste Land*, the scriptures of the East. He finds the same doctrine of response to what is always present in the *Bhagavad-Gita*.[1] There Arjuna is concerned with the problem of the innate sinfulness of human action, and Krishna replies to his doubts by insisting on the necessity of disinterestedness. Man must not look for the fruits of action; he must live as if there were no future, as if every moment were the moment of death. The New Testament teaches a similar carelessness for the morrow, which is echoed in *The Rock*:

I have said, take no thought of the harvest, but only of proper sowing.

The future is thought of here as something that already exists, as if it were a past we have not yet encountered, and

[1] Though it is perfectly in consonance with the poem's theme of annunciations to use these great scriptures which bear witness to man's recognition of the divine, it might be objected that to introduce Krishna at this point is an error and destroys the imaginative harmony of the poem, since it is precisely in their view of history and the time process that Christianity and Hinduism are most opposed. I imagine that the reason for the introduction of the *Gita* here is that the poem contains so much of Mr Eliot's past that inevitably his explorations of Hindu metaphysics find a place in it. He has owned that two years' study of Sanskrit and 'a year in the mazes of Patanjali's metaphysics' left him 'in a state of enlightened mystification', and I must own that is the feeling the passage leaves me with. It is introduced rather tentatively, as a piece of speculation.

the image of passengers appears now again. But the passengers are no longer in the underground; they are journeying in the open air, on a long train journey and later on a sea voyage. The oppression of the first two poems has lifted. First in a train, then on the ocean, the travellers fare forward, bearing their past with them and their future also. In a real sense they are between two lives; yet to divide time harshly, into past, present and future, is to divide ourselves, to disintegrate personality:

> You are not the same people who left that station
> Or who will arrive at any terminus.

Personality has meaning only in the present, in what we are. Our real destination is here; where we are going is where we are.[1]

The lyrical fourth movement is a prayer to Our Lady, and its tender gravity and perfect fitness illustrate the unity in the poem between idea and symbol. She is rightly prayed to in a poem of the sea, because she is 'Stella Maris' to whom the fishermen and their wives pray. She appears also at the poem's lyrical climax as the handmaid of the Lord, who made the great response to the message of the angel, and as the Mother of Christ, whose birth gives meaning to time. She is also prayed to as Mater Dolorosa, for this is a poem of sorrows, and the whole lyric takes up the theme of the lovely melancholy sestina of the second movement; it recalls the dangerous voyages, the ocean 'littered with wastage', and over all

[1] It is worth noting that the phrase

> this thing is sure,
> That time is no healer: the patient is no longer here,

echoes Pascal, while contradicting him: 'Le temps guérit les douleurs et les querelles, parce qu'on change, on n'est plus la même personne. Ni l'offensant, ni l'offensé, ne sont plus eux-mêmes' (*Pensées*, II, 122). Earlier in the same section Pascal had asserted the persistence of personality: 'Tout ce qui se perfectionne par progrès périt aussi par progrès, tout ce qui a été faible ne peut jamais être absolument fort. On a beau dire: *il est crû il est changé*; il est aussi le même' (II, 88).

the sound of the sea-bell's
Perpetual angelus.

The fifth movement opens with a topical passage on the theme of men's attitudes to the past and the future, which they peer into for comfort and guidance. They turn to fortune-tellers and astrologers for re-assurance about the future which they dread, like the 'anxious worried women' of the first movement, or they turn to the past to explain the present:

Men's curiosity searches past and future
And clings to that dimension.

Opposed to this search into past and future is the occupation of the saint, the attempt to apprehend

The point of intersection of the timeless
With time.

For the ordinary man who is not a saint there are moments of illumination: 'hints and guesses, hints followed by guesses', on which he founds his life of 'prayer, observance, discipline, thought and action'. In these apprehensions of the eternal, preserved in memory and fruitful beyond the moment in which they were first felt, we find freedom from the tyranny of past and future, and cease to feel ourselves the helpless victims of natural forces. Because of this inner freedom, we can accept our temporal destiny and our bond with nature, the 'dung and death' to which 'our temporal reversion' must return. In the 'hint half guessed, the gift half understood' we find not only the meaning of our own lives, but also the purpose of history. Thus time is redeemed and is seen to be no enemy; for in time the world was made, in time God was and is manifested in Incarnation, and as Blake asserted in his *Marriage of Heaven and Hell*: 'Eternity is in love with the productions of time.'

The subject of *The Dry Salvages* in the literal sense is

again not a particular experience, but the sum of experiences we call the past, our own past and the past of the human race: in a word, history. Unlike the other Quartets it has no break in its third movement, and there is in it not a turn, but a change of feeling. Although the poem as a whole speaks of the past, here the subject becomes the future; but it is the future felt in the present, as the past is known in the present. The subject of the poem in the moral sense is hope, and this is apparent in the change of tone in the third movement. This hope is not the hope that the future will somehow be different from the past, or that we shall escape from ourselves and be in some way different in the future. It is a present hope: the hope of our calling, the noble virtue which Crashaw defended against Cowley:

> True Hope's a glorious Huntresse, and her chase
> The God of Nature in the field of Grace.

This hope renews the world, and allows the poet to feel that the world of nature is the field of grace. In the mystical sense the subject of the poem is the Incarnation, through which time is united to eternity. All the annunciations of the poem have validity through the one Annunciation.

In contrast with *The Dry Salvages*, which is peopled by the anonymous, the fishermen 'forever bailing, setting and hauling', the 'anxious worried women lying awake', the passengers settling for a journey, *Little Gidding* is full of particular destinies. The setting of the poem has a historical not a personal significance, and place and time are exactly defined. It is 'while the light fails on a winter's afternoon, in a secluded chapel'. The poem is the record of a visit with a deliberate purpose: 'You are here to kneel where prayer has been valid.' We are not concerned with the 'hints and guesses' of the earlier poems, but with the life of 'prayer, observance, discipline, thought and action'. The actions of men, particularly their political actions, all that area of experience in which we are most aware of our freedom, are the subject of meditation, things done rather than things suffered and endured. The thought of sin occurs for the first time, not the sickness of the soul as in *East Coker*, but actual sin: 'things ill done and done to others' harm.'

Little Gidding is a place of dedication, to which people came with purpose. It was not the ancestral home of the Ferrars, but a house which old Mrs Ferrar had bought and to which the family retired during the plague of 1625. In the next year Nicholas Ferrar 'grew to a full Resolution and determination of that thing and course of life he had so often wished for and longingly desired. And that week before Whitsonday gave himself to a very private Retirement, both in his thoughts and in his person, and was observed to fast much, eate sparingly and sleep little, and on Whitson Eve he was up all night in his Study.' On Trinity Sunday he went with his tutor to see Laud, and was ordained deacon, refusing all his life to proceed to the priesthood, and returned to Little Gidding to share his goods with his family and lead that life of ordered devotion and good works which made this remote Huntingdonshire village famous throughout England. An admirable picture of the life at Little Gidding can be found in Shorthouse's novel *John Inglesant*. It is a book of singular charm and refinement of feeling and all that is necessary for an understanding of what the name of the poem should suggest can be found in it. King Charles visited the community in 1633, and again during the troubled year of 1642, and legend says he came there for shelter by night, 'a broken king', after the final defeat of his cause at Naseby, just before he went north to give himself up to the Scots. Little Gidding is then a place of defeat. The community was scattered in 1647 and the chapel left ruined, and though the chapel was restored for worship in the nineteenth century, Nicholas Ferrar's ideal of a religious community based on the Christian family was never revived in the Anglican Church. Little Gidding remains 'a symbol perfected in death'.

The first movement of the poem is in three parts, but the transitions are not abrupt, and the third part is a kind of recapitulation or development of the second, opening with the same phrase, but at the close recurring to the image of fire from the first. The first paragraph gives a vivid impression of 'midwinter spring', the season that is 'not in time's covenant', a time of 'frost and fire' and 'blossom of snow' It is shot through with the sense of something given, uncovenanted, and miraculous. The second paragraph asserts human purpose. It declares that at any time or any season this is a place of destiny, where the purpose with which men come is changed; while the third brings us to the particular purpose of the poet here, which is prayer, and to the thought of the dead whose communication 'is tongued with fire beyond the language of the living'. The place is both England and nowhere; a place we have come to deliberately at a certain moment, and a place where we find ourselves outside place and time.

The beautiful lyric on decay and disintegration and death which opens the second movement recalls the imagery of the earlier poems. The 'burnt roses' and the 'dust in the air suspended' are from *Burnt Norton*, the 'wall, the wainscot and the mouse' from *East Coker*, the 'dead water and dead sand' from *The Dry Salvages*. The symbolism of the four elements which runs through *Four Quartets* here reaches its fullest expression. The effect of the lyric is cumulative; human emotion and human passion depart into the air, human effort crumbles into dust, the monuments of the human spirit are rotted by the corrosion of water and fire. The disintegration into the four elements whose mysterious union makes life finds its most poignant symbol in the final image of the gutted and water-logged ruins of 'sanctuary and choir'.

This theme of the 'death of hope and despair' and of the 'vanity of toil' underlies the colloquy that follows. Whereas in the other poems this section is a meditation, here, in keeping with the historical subject, we have an episode; a particular moment in time described. It is at dawn, between the departure of the last bomber and the sounding of the All Clear, and the scene is the streets of London. Instead of the poet's own reflections we have the conversation with the 'dead master', a communication from one whose 'concern was speech', and who in his day had his own 'thought and theory'. The setting, the style, and above all the metre, at once suggest *The Divine Comedy*. The stranger has the 'brown baked features' of Brunetto Latini (*Inferno xv*), and he ends his speech with the thought of the 'refining fire' of the *Purgatorio*, while his melancholy sense of supersession: 'Last season's fruit is eaten', recalls the words of Oderisi (*Purgatorio xi*). But although the *Comedy* is full of interviews such as this, and in spite of the Dantean imagery and reminiscences, we are not to identify this 'familiar compound ghost' with Dante or with any other single poet. The ghost is 'both one and many'; he is 'intimate and unidentifiable'; he speaks of the experience of the poet in all ages and the fact that he adapts a line from Mallarmé,[1] and appears to recall a famous phrase of Virgil's seems to depersonalize him rather than to suggest any identification. But the tone of the speech and some of the phrases recall strongly one great English poet, and that is Milton, the Milton of the close of *Paradise Lost*, of *Paradise Regained* and of *Samson Agonistes*. When we hear the disclosure of 'the

---

[1] 'Donner un sens plus pur aux mots de la tribu' ('Le Tombeau d'Edgar Poe'). I take it that the line 'When I left my body on a distant shore' is a periphrasis for dying, the distant shore being the *ulterior ripa* of Virgil.

gifts reserved for age' we remember Milton's melancholy picture of old age:

> Thou must outlive
> Thy youth, thy strength, thy beauty, which will change
> To withered weak and gray; thy Senses then
> Obtuse, all taste of pleasure must forgoe,
> To what thou hast.

And the close of the speech has a haunting Miltonic echo. 'I cannot praise a fugitive and cloistered virtue *unexercised* and unbreathed', wrote the confident Milton of 1644. The mood is very different and deeply troubled in *Paradise Regained* when political action is considered and in *Samson Agonistes* where 'patience is the *exercise* of saints'. The human suffering in Milton's later poetry, a touch of the scorn with which he cries: 'What is glory but the blaze of fame', and the patience of his spirit seem to be suggested by this conversation in the disfigured streets of London:

> First, the cold friction of expiring sense
> Without enchantment, offering no promise
> But bitter tastelessness of shadow fruit
> As body and soul begin to fall asunder.
> Second, the conscious impotence of rage
> At human folly, and the laceration
> Of laughter at what ceases to amuse.
> And last, the rending pain of re-enactment
> Of all that you have done, and been; the shame
> Of motives late revealed, and the awareness
> Of things ill done and done to others' harm
> Which once you took for exercise of virtue.
> Then fools' approval stings, and honour stains.

Indeed Milton, whom Mr Eliot confesses he finds so antipathetic as a man, is very much in mind throughout the poem. The reference is explicit in the next section where along with Strafford, Laud and Charles, who died on the scaffold, the poet remembers 'one who died blind and quiet',[1]

---

[1] 'Hee dy'd', wrote Milton's earliest biographer, 'in a fitt of the Gout, but with so little pain or Emotion, that the time of his expiring was not

and though the words are not Milton's the repeated 'all shall be well' reminds us of the conclusion of Milton's last poem, the final chorus of *Samson Agonistes*:

> All is best, though we oft doubt,
> What th'unsearchable dispose
> Of highest wisdom brings about,
> And ever best found in the close.

After the grave melancholy of the second movement the third opens with a tone of confidence and in a rhythm that is almost gay. The beautiful imagery of the first movement is recalled in the metaphor of the hedgerow, and the change in human beings from attachment to detachment is thus felt to be something natural, occurring in the proper course of things. Between these two states, 'unflowering', is the detachment of the Stoics or of the Gnostic *illuminati*, the sterile apparent freedom from desire of those who have never felt love. These reflections on the pattern of our individual lives yield to the thought of the pattern of history, where we can feel a unity between men who in a 'warlike various and tragical age' found themselves opposed. At the turn of the movement and again at its close, and at the close of the whole poem, which is also the close of the sequence, Mr Eliot has set the mysterious words of Julian of Norwich, which sum up the discovery of the poem.[1]

---

perceiv'd by those in the room. And though hee had bin long troubl'd with that disease, insomuch that his knuckles were all callous, yet was hee not ever observ'd to be very impatient.' Although the Miltonic reference seems to me primary, it is possible that the poet had also in mind the death of James Joyce who had died recently 'abroad'.

[1] Whether he was aware of it or not, Mr Eliot's use of Dame Julian is highly appropriate, for the medieval English mystics were much loved in the seventeenth century, particularly by those who 'died forgotten in other places abroad'—the exiled Romanists. Dame Julian was printed in a modernized edition in 1670 by Serenus de Cressy, once Fellow of Merton and Chaplain to Falkland, later a Benedictine at Douai. Cressy appears in *John Inglesant* at a moving moment in the story to urge on Inglesant the claims of the monastic life.

Dame Julian, whom some think the greatest of the medieval English mystics, received sixteen 'shewings' in the year 1373, which she wrote down and amplified and explained fifteen years later. Her Revelations were of the Passion and of words spoken to her from the Cross. In her Thirteenth Revelation she was much troubled by the thought of the origin of sin in a world created by infinite Goodness, but the voice which spoke to her said: 'Sin is behovely, but all shall be well, and all shall be well, and all manner of thing shall be well'; and in her Fourteenth Revelation concerning prayer she heard the words: 'I am Ground of thy Beseeching.' For fifteen years, as she tells us, she pondered on the meaning of what she had heard and seen, and she was at last answered: 'Wouldst thou learn thy Lord's meaning in this thing? Learn it well: Love was His meaning. Who shewed it thee? Love. What shewed He thee? Love. Wherefore shewed it He? For Love. Hold thee therein and thou shalt learn and know more in the same. But thou shalt never know or learn therein other thing without end.'

This Love is the theme of the lyric movement. The fires which have flamed and glowed throughout the poem here break out and declare their nature. Man cannot help loving; his choice is between the fire of self-love and the fire of the love of God. The 'dark disordered fire of our soul', wrote William Law, 'can as well be made the foundation of Heaven as it is of Hell. For when the fire and strength of the soul is sprinkled with the blood of the Lamb, then its fire becomes a fire of light, and its strength is changed into a strength of triumphing love, and will be fitted to have a place among those flames of love that wait about the throne of God.' As *East Coker* has at this point a lyric on the eternal Passion, *Little Gidding* celebrates the eternal Pentecost, the perpetual descent of the Dove in tongues of fire.

The assurance and serenity of the final movement

crown the whole sequence. The line dividing its two paragraphs, which comes from the second chapter of *The Cloud of Unknowing*:

With the drawing of this Love and the voice of this Calling,

makes explicit the meaning of the 'moment in the rose-garden', the bell heard beneath the waves, and the 'communication of the dead'. History is the field of the operation of the Spirit; it is a 'pattern of timeless moments'. The historic moment, the moment of choice is always here. We are back again at the close in the garden of *Burnt Norton*, passing through the first gate into our first world, and the children are there in the apple-tree. Effort and exploration are forgotten in the sense of the given; living is the discovery of the already known, and beginning and end are one. All shall be well, when all is gathered in love, and the rose, the symbol of natural beauty and natural love, is one with the fire, the love by which all things are made. *Little Gidding* is a poem of fire, the fire which is torment to the self-loving, purgation to the penitent, and ecstasy to the blessed, and it closes with mortal and immortal life united in the resurrection symbol of the rose of heaven. 'And I saw full surely', wrote Dame Julian at the close of her book, 'that ere God made us He loved us; which love was never slacked, nor ever shall be. And in this love He hath done all His works; and in this love is our life everlasting. In our making we had beginning; but the love wherein He made us was in Him without beginning: in which love we have our beginning. And all this shall we see in God without end.'

The subject of *Little Gidding* in the literal sense is a visit to the chapel there, on a winter's afternoon, in order to pray in a place made holy by the prayers of other men. More generally, the literal subject is all such purposeful action, which has purpose

> beyond the end you figured
> And is altered in fulfilment.

In the moral sense, the subject is charity, 'the very bond of peace and of all virtues, without which whosoever liveth is counted dead': the

> expanding
> Of love beyond desire.

In the mystical sense the subject is the Holy Spirit, the gift of the risen and ascended Lord. But when we reach *Little Gidding* we see the total subject emerge. In the literal sense it is consciousness, the faculty by which man, living in time, transcends time, and stands outside process:

> To be conscious is not to be in time.

In the moral sense it is love, including in itself all other virtues, and in the mystical sense it is Love also, 'which is both the Giver and the Gift'.[1] Because consciousness within the poem becomes increasingly the consciousness of the past within the present, the consciousness finally of history, the subject, as the poem proceeds, finds its definition increasingly in the historic Christian terms. We can then say, finally, that mystically the subject of each poem and of the whole poem is Christ, Alpha and Omega, the Beginning and the End, Author and Finisher of our Faith.

Mr Eliot has always been a poet of vision. His earlier poetry presented mainly what Wordsworth called a 'visionary dreariness'. He might indeed be accused in his early poetry, as Mary accused Harry, of attaching himself to loathing as others do to loving. The effort of every true

[1] This phrase is from the second book of Walter Hilton's *Scale of Perfection*. Although he has not the lyrical fervour of Rolle, or the speculative genius of the author of *The Cloud of Unknowing*, or the theological insight of Dame Julian, Hilton has a depth of wisdom which makes his 'heavenly book more precious than gold'. The temper of *Little Gidding* is to me very near the temper of the second book of *The Scale of Perfection*.

poet is to unify his experience, and the development of every great poet is the extension of the amount of experience he can order into poetry. Mr Eliot could not have written *Four Quartets* if he had not earlier written 'Mr Eliot's Sunday Morning Service', where faith and hope and love are known in terms of their opposites. But the experience which lies behind *The Hollow Men* and *Ash Wednesday* compelled him to contemplate another vision: 'the visionary gleam, the glory and the dream', whose felt absence was his earlier subject. A deepening sense of the horror of life, something more terrible than dreariness, makes urgent the question; not why are we desolate, but why were we ever happy, or why did we ever expect happiness? Our wretchedness is not an illusion; was our joy, however transitory, perhaps equally real? After *The Waste Land* Mr Eliot's poetry becomes the attempt to find meaning in the whole of his experience, to include all that he has known. To do this, he enters into himself, finding within himself his own music and his own language.

English poetry is particularly rich in visionary poets: Langland, Vaughan, Traherne, Smart, Blake, Wordsworth. But these are not the poets we think of when we think of Mr Eliot. Although he shares with them the power to render 'unknown modes of Being', he differs from them in his attitude to the poet's task. His unique distinction among English poets is the balance he has maintained between the claims of his vision and the claims of his art. In his poetry he is neither a prophet nor a visionary primarily, but a poet, a great 'maker'. When we read *Four Quartets* we are left finally not with the thought of 'the transitory Being who beheld this vision', nor with the thought of the vision itself, but with the poem, beautiful, satisfying, self-contained, self-organized, complete. His master in this is not an English poet, but the greatest of European poets of vision: Dante.

Although the range and scope of *The Divine Comedy* forbid us to make a comparison, yet there is a sense in which Mr Eliot can without impropriety be named with Dante. He too has found a 'dolce stil nuovo', and the origin of that style he could explain in Dante's words:

> Io mi son un che, quando
> amor mi spira, noto, ed a quel modo
> che ditta dentro, vo significando.